FACE TO FACE

FACE TO FACE

Meditations on the Life Everlasting

G. Thompson Brown

Geneva Press
Louisville, Kentucky

Book design by Sharon Adams
Cover design by Pam Poll Graphic Design

First edition

Published by Geneva Press
Louisville, Kentucky

This book is printed on acid-free paper that meets the American National Standards Institute Z39.48 standard. ∞

PRINTED IN THE UNITED STATES OF AMERICA

01 02 03 04 05 06 07 08 09 10 — 10 9 8 7 6 5 4 3 2 1

Library of Congress Cataloging-in-Publication Data is on file at the Library of Congress, Washington, D.C.

ISBN 0-664-50163-X

Contents

vi Contents

Acknowledgments

*I*t is a pleasure to express my thanks to those who were of help in the writing and the preparation of the text for publication. Because of the many references and quotes from many sources, this book could never have been written without the kind permissions to quote from the works of others. I wish to express special thanks to the following: Ben Johnson, my colleague and Professor of Spirituality at Columbia Seminary, for reading the manuscript and offering valuable advice; to Miriam Dunson, PCUSA Staff Associate for Older Adult Leadership Development, who supported this project which she felt would be a useful tool for those who work with retired people and those in nursing homes; to Rex Knowles for the use of his poem "Before the Lord"; to Wang Weifan for permission to quote a portion of his "Song of the Road Home"; to Richard Avery for his "Every Morning is Easter Morning from Now On"; to Jasper Keith, our pastor at Decatur Presbyterian, for tracking down the source of St. Augustine's "Happiness of the Heavenly Alleluia." Peter Kreeft's book *Everything You Wanted to Know about Heaven but Never Dreamed of Asking* was most helpful in understanding the Roman Catholic tradition. Other "permissions" are included on the copyright page.

A more personal word of thanks goes to members of our family: to my daughter, Charlotte Hill, for the story of the woman who wanted to be buried with the spoon in her hand; to my grandson, David, who copied the text of the "Merger" poem; and to my wife, Mardia, who read every line of the manuscript and picked up errors that Spell Check had missed.

I am grateful for the professional expertise of Geneva Press at all stages of the publication process, and I wish to express a special word of thanks for the support and guidance of Senior Consulting Editor Tom Long and for the careful proofreading and helpful changes suggested by Project Editor Daniel Braden.

Introduction

The idea for this book began when my wife Mardia, who is a Presbyterian elder, and I were asked to serve on a team that took communion to elderly members of our church, the Decatur (Georgia) Presbyterian Church. They were shut-ins, at home alone or confined to nursing homes or other places of long-term care. We were asked to make our visits once a quarter.

I had only two years' experience as a pastor of a local church before going to Korea as a missionary, and I was not prepared for what followed. Quite frankly, I was overwhelmed by the sight of the empty faces of people who seemed to have nothing to which they could look forward. Their lives seemed to be monotonous at best. Sometimes they were sedated to keep away the aches and pains. They spent long hours of the days and nights alone, full of anxieties about their future. The constant visible presence of wheelchairs, walkers, and the gear the nursing home used to keep its occupants alive didn't help. Some people reached out to us as complete strangers, wanting to tell their story, seeking a smile, some sign of cheer, or some word of recognition. Yes, some of these brave souls struggled to find meaning in their day-to-day existence. Would it help if they had a clearer image of their heavenly home?

Here were people who had served the Church of

Jesus Christ all their lives. Were we failing them in their time of need when they were coming to the end of their earthly sojourn? Where was "the sure and certain hope of the Resurrection"? These words would be read at their funerals, but what about now when the people needed this assurance most? Is heaven a subject that should be dodged whenever possible, except at funerals when it can't be avoided? Are we too much like the English vicar, who when asked by a colleague what he expected after death, replied: "Well, if it comes to that, I suppose I shall enter into eternal bliss, but I really wish you wouldn't bring up such depressing subjects"? (Peter Kreeft, *Everything You Ever Wanted to Know about Heaven but Never Dreamed of Asking,* 196.)

What words of support do we have for the caregivers whose ministry calls for great patience, sacrifice, and love? What can we say about eternal life that would bring meaning and purpose to those who minister to the patients of Alzheimer's disease or AIDS, whose future seems so bleak? I was at a loss in knowing how to minister to these precious ones who, as one of them put it, "found no light at the end of the tunnel." Serving communion was certainly the place to begin. But what to say next?

Seeking answers, I was driven back to search the Scriptures. I should not have been surprised at the rich treasury of hope, assurance, victory, joy, and peace that I found in every book of the New Testament and many places in the Old Testament. Jesus speaks of "heaven" often—at least seven times in the Sermon on the Mount. Biblical images speak with confidence of the state of the future life: trumpets, home, the banquet, rest, the city, the garden, rewards, children, friends, choirs, and the great white throne. To be sure, these images should not be taken literally, but they bear witness to a reality behind them. Could such images be gathered together in some meaningful pattern? Could verses of Scripture be put together not as proof texts but as words to ponder, to explore, and to meditate on during the long watches of a sleepless night?

Another surprise: Near unanimity of the witness to the Resurrection and the future life can be found in the creeds of Christendom. Nicea, The Apostles' Creed, Westminster, and Heidelberg all speak of the same faith with the same voice. Some differences among these creeds exist, but the central fact of the Resurrection of Jesus Christ and the life everlasting are never in dispute. I found a great treasury of faith and hope in the life eternal in the writings of the saints and sages, the prophets and poets, hymn writers and common Christian folk down through the centuries. Some are mystical, some philosophical, some down to earth, some fanciful and imaginative, some even humorous. Some are to be sung, some pondered, some to be explored, some committed to memory. Some call for praise and thanksgiving, some for repentance, some for intercession. Here is the faith countless Christians of all persuasions (Roman Catholic, Protestant, and Orthodox) have lived by and that has supported them when they faced death. Previous generations have been far less reticent than our own to speak of the future life.

Some people charge that an emphasis on the future life is a form of escapism designed to avoid the cares and concerns of this present world: the old Marxist critique of "pie in the sky by-and-by." I found that the biblical witness simply does not support this view. The biblical formula is never "heaven" or "earth" exclusively but always "heaven and earth." Each time we pray the Lord's Prayer, we commit ourselves to the coming of the kingdom here "on earth as it is in heaven." Belief in the future life has been a strong motivating force for addressing, here and now, the ills of society. Having made our peace with the future, we are freed up to find meaning and purpose and joy in this world today, whatever its changing scene and vicissitudes.

So the format of this little book began to emerge. I would

put together thirty-one meditations. Perhaps they could be used one a day for each day of the month. Each meditation would be based on a biblical image that speaks of heaven or the future life. Each devotion would be divided into three sections:

(1) Some passages of Scripture that related to the image under consideration for that day;
(2) a representative selection of Christian classics (both ancient and modern) that speak to the theme; and
(3) my own commentary, pulling together from my experience some thoughts for the day.

I do not try to argue or to debate the case for immortality. Rather, we would simply bear witness to what has been handed down to us and which we, the Christian community, have come to believe (1 Cor. 15:3). Adherents of other religions propose other views of the future life. Christians need to understand them and engage these people in dialogue. But that is not the purpose of this small volume, which is addressed to members of the Christian community.

Some people have no faith in a future life. To those we would say: Our role is not that of a judge. Our purpose here is much more modest. We simply wish to bear witness to the faith that is within us. We believe that it makes sense, and we commend it to any reader for consideration. We have no desire to become involved with speculation about the millennium, but the book might be read by those seeking a sane understanding of the biblical view of heaven and the future life.

Belief in the life eternal is not easy. In perhaps no other article of our faith do we so clearly contradict the prevailing secularism of the culture of today. We see through a glass darkly (1 Cor. 13:12). Our minds cannot penetrate the frontiers of time and space. "Hope that is seen is not hope" (Rom. 8:24, NRSV).

We simply rest our case on the Resurrection of Jesus Christ. "If for this life only we have hoped in Christ, we are of all people most to be pitied" (1 Cor. 15:19, NRSV). But let's not jump ahead of the story, for the Resurrection is where we begin with Day 1. . . .

Chapter 1

Easter People

I am the resurrection and the life. Those who believe in me, even though they die, will live, and everyone who lives and believes in me will never die. (John 11:25–26, NRSV)

. . . I handed on to you as of first importance what I in turn had received: that Christ died for our sins in accordance with the scriptures, and that he was buried, and that he was raised on the third day in accordance with the scriptures, and that he appeared to Cephas, then to the twelve. Then he appeared to more than five hundred brothers and sisters at one time. . . . so we proclaim and so you have come to believe. . . . If Christ has not been raised, your faith is futile. . . . If for this life only we have hoped in Christ, we are of all people most to be pitied. But in fact Christ has been raised. . . . "Death has been swallowed up in victory." "Where, O death, is your victory? Where, O death, is your sting?" . . . Thanks be to God, who gives us the victory through our Lord Jesus Christ. (1 Cor. 15:3–57, NRSV)

• • •

I believe in one God the Father Almighty . . . And in one Lord Jesus Christ . . . Who for us men and for our salvation came down from heaven, and was incarnate by the Holy Ghost of the Virgin Mary, And was made man: And was crucified also for us under

Pontius Pilate; He suffered and was buried: And the third day he rose again according to the Scriptures: And ascended into heaven, And sitteth at the right hand of the Father: And he shall come again, with glory to judge both the quick and the dead. . . . And I look for the resurrection of the dead and the life of the world to come. (Nicene Creed, 325 A.D.)

If it could be shown as clear historical evidence that the bones of Jesus had moldered away in a Palestinian grave like the bones of any other man, I would cease to be a worshipping Christian. (Stephen Neill, church historian)

To say "Jesus is alive" means that Jesus is a living person just as I am a living person. It means that on that first Easter more than 1,900 years ago the tomb in which Jesus' friends had laid his crucified body was empty. God raised him from the dead, and during the forty days before his Ascension, Jesus appeared in bodily form to his disciples just as the Scriptures say. . . . If Jesus is not alive—if his body is still in the tomb . . . If for this life only we have hoped in Christ, we are of all persons most to be pitied. (Ben Lacy Rose, *Presbyterian Survey*)

I think that the resurrection of Jesus is in some way what makes Christianity meaningful. . . . What I want to emphasize here is that I believe that Christianity could have no basis at all if it were not for this resurrection. . . . When we read about Christ in his life before his death, it absolutely makes no sense whatsoever unless something else beyond this happened—unless the resurrection occurred. . . . (Frank A. Brown Jr., brother of the author and medical missionary to Japan in a family letter shortly before his death, 1980)

Christianity stands or falls with the reality of the raising of Jesus from the dead by God. In the New Testament there is no faith that does not start a priori with the resurrection of Jesus. . . . A Christian faith that is not resurrection faith can therefore be called neither Christian nor faith. (Jurgen Moltman, *The Theology of Hope,* 166)

• • •

"Every morning is Easter morning from now on. . . ." This line from the chorus by Richard Avery and Donald Marsh says it all. The Easter event is the decisive event for every day in the year. The New Testament message is clear. The evidence is overwhelming. The apostle Paul rests the entire case for Christianity on the resurrection of Jesus Christ. All the ancient creeds of the church are unanimous in affirming the centrality of the Easter message of hope and victory. Today, Christians from every continent—theologians, priests, pastors, missionaries, and lay people—have found that faith in the resurrection of Jesus Christ brings meaning and purpose in their daily lives. Common Christian folk have bet their future in this life and in the life to come on this one central fact of history. This faith is the one unifying mark of what it means to be Christian.

Some years ago I hailed a taxi at the railroad station in Seoul, Korea, and as I got in, I gave the driver my destination. Immediately he asked, "You are a foreigner, yet you are speaking in Korean. Who are you, anyway?" This inquiry started a conversation. We were passing through some of the worst traffic of the city, and each time he spoke he turned his head and took his eyes off the road. You can understand why my answers were short and to the point!

"I am an American. I live here."

"Why did you come to Korea?"

"I am a missionary."

"So, you are a Christian."

"Yes."

"I am a Buddhist. My wife is better at it than I am. I don't have time because I am driving the taxi every day. Say, what is the chief difference between Buddhism and Christianity?"

Here was no time for a discussion of comparative religion. My answer had to be in language the taxicab driver could understand, using the simple Korean words that I knew. My response: "The chief difference between Buddhism and Christianity is that we believe that Jesus Christ rose from the dead."

"Do you really believe that?"

"Yes."

Then it was my turn to ask a question. "What do you believe about life, death, and resurrection?"

He gave a shrug of the shoulders and repeated a typically Korean expression, "*Kulsi.* Who knows?"

My response: "We believe that not only did Jesus rise from the dead but that he is alive and with us today."

We were at my destination. The conversation was at an end. Just possibly the driver had found another option for life.

The Resurrection gave me something to share with the Seoul taxicab driver. If it wasn't for the Resurrection I would have had nothing to say. There would have been no point in my going to Korea or staying there twenty years.

Some years ago on an Easter Sunday in Russia, the Atheist League was holding a rally in a public square. At the mass meeting, speaker after speaker came to the podium and presented evidence against the existence of God and the deity of Christ. A Russian Orthodox priest came up to the platform and asked if he could say a few words. "Yes," said the presiding officer. "We have freedom of religion. Take two minutes." The priest replied that he would not need that long. He raised his arms in a blessing and repeated the ancient Easter greeting the Russian people exchange with each other on Easter Sunday:

"Christ is Risen."

That's all he said. And the great throng of people rose to their feet and repeated the traditional Easter response:

"He is Risen, Indeed."

Chapter 2

Keeper of the Keys

*T*hen Jesus . . . came to the tomb. It was a cave, and
a stone was lying against it. Jesus said, "Take away
the stone." . . . So they took away the stone. Then
Jesus looked upward and said, "Father, I thank you
for having heard me." . . . When he had said this, he
cried out with a loud voice, "Lazarus, come out!"
The dead man came out, his hands and feet bound
with strips of cloth, and his face wrapped in a cloth.
Jesus said to them, "Unbind him, and let him go."
(John 11:38–44, NRSV)

Fear not, I am the first and the last, and the living one;
I died, and behold I am alive for evermore, and I have
the keys of Death and Hades. (Rev. 1:17–18, RSV)

These are the words of the holy one, the true one,
   who has the key of David,
   who opens and no one will shut,
   who shuts and no one opens.
                    (Rev. 3:7, NRSV)

• • •

Death, be not proud, though some have called thee
Mighty and dreadful, for thou are not so:

For those whom thou think'st thou dost overthrow
Die not, poor Death; nor yet canst thou kill me. . . .

One short sleep past, we wake eternally,
And Death shall be no more: Death, thou shalt die!
                (John Donne, 1573–1631)

God's Kingdom cannot fail
Christ rules over earth and heaven
The keys of death and hell
Are to our Jesus given.
Lift up your hearts! Lift up your voice!
Rejoice; Again I say, Rejoice!
                    (Charles Wesley, 1764)

• • •

The scene was at the waiting room of the hospital's intensive care unit. The coffee was stale and tasteless. The magazines were outdated, and the newspapers were of little interest. Tubes and wires connected the loved one to the respirator, gauges, and machines. The family had gathered. Decisions had to be made. What were we to do?

I thought of two passages of Scripture. The first was that magnificent passage from the eleventh chapter of John, when Jesus stands before the tomb of Lazarus and gives commands to family, friends, and the dead man: "Lazarus, come out! . . . Unbind him and let him go" (John 11:43–44, NRSV). The second comes from the Revelation when the risen, living Lord addresses the church and says, "I have the keys of Death and Hades" (Rev. 1:18, RSV).

The living Lord Jesus is the "Keeper of the Keys," not blind fate, chance, or bad luck. The keys do not reside in the machines in the intensive care unit. The Lord holds the keys, and he does not delegate that responsibility to anyone else. He stands between the loved one and the tomb. When he says "Open," it opens, and when he says "Close," it closes.

Sometimes he stands on this side of the tomb, as he did before the tomb of Lazarus, and commands, "Lazarus, come out." Death is powerless to stop him. Death, humbled and obedient, opens the gate and Lazarus comes forth. The graveclothes no longer bind him. Lazarus is free again.

And sometimes the living Lord stands on the other side of

the tomb. He is still the Keeper of the Keys. He calls out with a loud voice, "Joe, come out. It's better for you now to be with me on this side." And Death is powerless to hold him. Death, humbled and obedient, opens the gate and Joe crosses over. The trappings of the intensive care unit are no longer needed. The infirmities of stroke, sickness, and age disappear. Joe is whole and free again.

Chapter 3

River Jordan

*W*hen you pass through the waters, I will be with
    you;
    and through the rivers, they shall not overwhelm
    you;
when you walk through fire you shall not be
    burned,
    and the flame shall not consume you.
For I am the LORD your God,
    the Holy One of Israel, your Savior.
                     (Is. 43:2–3, NRSV)

• • •

Now I further saw that betwixt them and the Gate
was a River, but there was no Bridge to go over, the
River was very deep: at the sight therefore of this
River the Pilgrims were much stunned; but the men
that went with them said, You must go through, or
you cannot come to the Gate. . . . The Pilgrims then,
especially Christian, began to despond in his mind,
and looked this way and that, but no way could be
found by them by which they might escape the River.
Then they asked the men if the Waters were all of a
depth? They said . . . "you shall find it deeper or shallower, as you believe in the King of the place."

Then they addressed themselves to the Water; and
entering, Christian began to sink, and crying out to
his good friend Hopeful, he said, I sink in deep
Water; the Billows go over my head, all his Waves go
over me. . . .

Then said the other (Hopeful), Be of good cheer my Brother, I feel the bottom and it is good. Then said Christian, Ah my friend, the sorrows of death have compassed me about, I shall not see the land that flows with milk and honey. . . . He was much in the troublesome thoughts of the sins that he had committed, both since and before he began to be a Pilgrim. . . . Hopeful therefore here had much ado to keep his Brother's head above water; yea sometimes he would be quite gone down, and then ere a while he would rise up again half dead. Hopeful also would endeavor to comfort him, saying Brother, I see the Gate, and men standing by to receive us. But Christian would answer, 'tis you, 'tis you they wait for, you have been hopeful ever since I knew you. . . .

Then I saw in my dream that Christian was as in a muse a while. To whom also Hopeful added this word, "Be of good cheer, Jesus Christ maketh thee whole." And with that Christian broke out with a loud voice, O I see him again, and he tells me, "When thou passest through the Waters, I will be with thee; and through the Rivers, they shall not overflow thee." Then they both took courage, and the Enemy was after that as still as a stone, until they were gone over. . . . (John Bunyan, *Pilgrim's Progress,* 149–50)

> When I trod the verge of Jordan
> Bid my anxious fears subside
> Death of death and Hell's Destruction
> Land me safe on Canaan's side
> Strong Deliverer, Strong Deliverer
> Be thou still my Strength and Shield
> Be thou still my Strength and Shield.
> (William Williams, 1745)

> When through the deep waters I call thee to go
> The rivers of sorrow shall not overflow;
> For I will be near thee
> Thy troubles to bless,
> And sanctify to thee thy deepest distress.
> (John Rippon, 1787)

• • •

In Christian symbolism, the image of death is the Jordan River. It is not the Pit, Sheol, or the shadowy abode of the dead. It is a river and rivers are for crossing. Rivers serve as boundaries between two realms. In the case of the Jordan, it's the boundary between the dry, arid land of the wilderness and the "land flowing with milk and honey."

In John Bunyan's allegory, *Pilgrim's Progress,* note the rich symbolism of Christian's crossing of the "River." It cannot be avoided. But for some the river is deeper and for others it is shallower depending on one's faith in the "King of the place." Christian has a companion, Hopeful, who goes with him every step of the way. Hopeful brings cheer and comfort through the memory of Scripture passages. Hopeful keeps Christian's head just barely above the water. Hopeful feels the bottom, and it is firm and good. Just when it seems that Christian is sinking out of sight, weighted down by the memory of his sins, the promises of Jesus Christ lift him up. Then Hopeful sees the Gate on the other side. And beside the Gate those who have crossed over earlier have gathered to welcome the pilgrims. Even as Christian reached the deepest part of the river, a welcome was being prepared. For on the other side was the Promised Land.

> On Jordan's stormy bank I stand
> And cast a wishful eye
> To Canaan's fair and happy land
> Where my possessions lie.
> (Samuel Stennett 1727-1795)

Chapter 4

Trumpets

*A*ll the ends of the earth have seen
   the victory of our God.
Make a joyful noise to the LORD, all the earth;
   break forth into joyous song and sing praises.
Sing praises to the LORD with the lyre,
   with the lyre and the sound of melody.
With trumpets and the sound of the horn
   make a joyful noise before the King, the LORD.
                     (Ps. 98:3–6, NRSV)

And he will send out his angels with a loud trumpet
call, and they will gather his elect from the four
winds, from one end of heaven to the other. (Matt.
24:31, NRSV)

Lo! I tell you a mystery. We shall not all sleep, but
we shall all be changed, in a moment, in the twin-
kling of an eye, at the last trumpet. For the trumpet
will sound, and the dead will be raised imperishable,
and we shall be changed. (1 Cor. 15:51–52, RSV)

Then the seventh angel blew his trumpet, and there
were loud voices in heaven, saying, "The kingdom of
the world has become the kingdom of our Lord and
of his Christ, and he shall reign for ever and ever."
(Rev. 11:15, RSV)

Precious in the sight of the LORD is the death of his
faithful ones. (Psalm 116:15, NRSV)

• • •

The trumpet shall sound, and the dead shall be raised incorruptible, and we shall be changed. (Georg Friedrich Handel, 1685–1759, *Messiah*)

Thus they [Christian and Hopeful] got over [the River]. Now upon the bank of the River on the other side, they saw the two shining men, again who there waited for them: wherefore being come out of the River, they saluted them saying, "We are ministering Spirits, sent forth to minister for those that shall be heirs of salvation." . . . They had left their mortal Garments behind them in the River, for though they went in with them, they came out without them. . . . There came out also at this time to meet them, several of the King's Trumpeters, clothed in white and shining Raiment, who with melodious noises and loud, made even the Heaven to echo with their sound. These Trumpeters saluted Christian and his fellow with ten thousand welcomes from the World, and this they did with shouting and sound of trumpets. (Bunyan, *Pilgrim's Progress*, 151–53)

We begin with one immense fact. . . . The Christian belief is that after death individuality will survive, that you will still be you, and I will still be I. (William Barclay, *The Letters to the Corinthians*, 157)

• • •

Trumpets are for praising God. They speak decisively and with great authority. They are God's instruments for making a proclamation of victory or the announcement that some new thing is about to happen. In Scripture trumpets do not sound the plaintive notes of "Taps" but the rousing bugle call of "Reveille." A new day is about to begin.

Such a new day is described in Bunyan's vision of the river crossing. Just as Christian and his companion, Hopeful, were reaching the deepest point and near despair, the trumpeters were raising their trumpets in preparation for a mighty blast. And when the pilgrims came up out of the water, all the trumpets sounded! Ten thousand of them. It was Heaven's "twenty-one-gun salute" to the pilgrims who had safely crossed over. The successful crossing of the river by any one pilgrim is the cause of quite a celebration. God does not take lightly the death of any one of God's faithful ones. Each pilgrim is given a royal welcome.

Note that the crossing of the river does not change the identity of the pilgrim. Christian is still Christian. Hopeful is still Hopeful. There is a change though. Each will be given new garments to take the place of those left in the water. But the change does not mean that they lost their identity or surrendered their personalities. Each, freed from earthly handicaps and limitation, will be even more fully themselves.

Chapter 5

Amazing Grace

*T*o you, who were spiritually dead . . . to you Christ
has given life! . . . Even though we were dead in our
sins God who is rich in mercy because of the great
love he had for us gave us life together with Christ—
it is, remember, by grace and not by achievement that
you are saved—and has lifted us right out of the old
life to take our place with him in Christ Jesus in the
Heavens. Thus he shows for all time the tremendous
generosity of the grace and kindness he has
expressed toward us in Christ Jesus. It was nothing
you could do or achieve—it was God's gift of grace
which saved you. No one can pride himself upon
earning the love of God. The fact is that what we are
we owe to the hand of God upon us. (Eph. 2:1–9,
PHILLIPS)

We see Jesus, who for a little while was made lower
than the angels, crowned with glory and honor
because of the suffering of death, so that by the grace
of God he might taste death for everyone. (Heb. 2:9,
RSV)

• • •

Question: What is your only comfort, in life and in
death?
Answer: That I belong—body and soul, in life and
in death—not to myself but to my faithful Savior,

Jesus Christ, who at the cost of his own blood, has fully paid for all my sins and has completely freed me from the dominion of the devil; that he protects me so well that without the will of my Father in heaven not a hair can fall from my head; indeed, that everything must fit for his purpose for my salvation. Therefore by his Holy Spirit, he also assures me of eternal life, and makes me wholeheartedly willing and ready from now on to live for him. (Heidelberg Catechism, 1563)

"Through Grace Alone" . . . this is an extraordinarily consoling message which provides a solid basis for a man's life through all the inevitable failures, errors, and despair. And it frees that life also from the pressure to produce pious works, sustaining it through even the worst situations in freedom, wisdom, love, and hope. It is a message which need no longer be a matter of dispute between Catholic and Protestant theology. (Hans Kung, *On Being a Christian,* 408)

At the center of Jesus' parables of grace stands a God who takes the initiative toward us: a lovesick father who runs to meet the prodigal, a landlord who cancels a debt too large for any servant to reimburse, an employer who pays eleventh-hour workers the same as the first-hour crew, a banquet-giver who goes out to the highways and byways in search of undeserving guests. . . . God shatters the inexorable laws of sin and retribution by invading earth, absorbing the worst we had to offer, crucifixion, and then fashioning from that cruel deed the remedy for the human condition. Cavalry broke up the logjams between justice and forgiveness. By accepting onto his innocent self all the severe demands of justice, Jesus broke forever the chain of ungrace. (Philip Yancey, *What's So Amazing about Grace?,* 92)

Forgiveness breaks the chain of causality because he who "forgives" you—out of love—takes upon himself the consequences of what you have done. Forgiveness, therefore, always entails a sacrifice. The price you must pay for your own liberation through another's sacrifice is that you in turn must be willing to liberate in the same way, irrespective of the consequences to yourself. (Dag Hammarskjöld, *Markings,* 197)

Amazing Grace—how sweet the sound—That saved a
  wretch like me!
I once was lost, but now am found, Was blind, but now I
  see.

'Twas grace that taught my heart to fear, And grace my
  fears relieved;
How precious did that grace appear the hour I first
  believed.

Through many dangers, toils, and snares, I have already
  come;
'Tis grace has brought me safe thus far, and grace will
  lead me home.

When we've been there ten thousand years, Bright shining as the sun,
We've no less days, to sing God's praise than when we'd
  first begun.

(John Newton, 1779)

• • •

The River could never have been crossed if it had not been for God's amazing grace. What is so amazing about this grace? It's amazing because, "The notion of God's love coming to us free of charge, no strings attached, seems to go against every instinct of humanity" (Yancey, *What's So Amazing about Grace?,* 445). For the one who keeps the rules it is a scandal. Free and unlimited forgiveness is an unnatural act that runs counter to the normal way we think things ought to operate. And yet grace is the only thing that can reverse the inevitable decline of human activity into chaos and terror. Grace is the one thing that can bring to a halt the inescapable cycles of violence that make up human history. If the rule of "tit for tat" or "an eye for an eye and a tooth for a tooth" is allowed to run its course, there is simply no hope for the human race.

For Grace to have a chance, God must take the initiative: "in Christ God was reconciling the world to himself, not counting their trespasses against them" (2 Cor. 5:19, RSV). Grace is God's forgiveness raised to the nth degree. Such grace was costly beyond human imagination.

The popularity of John Newton's hymn seems strange for our times. The words are archaic and the imagery of a bygone day, yet no hymn has so captured the imagination of the American public. Folk-singers, entertainers, country music artists, young and old have picked up the familiar strains and the haunting melody. The words touch a cord that lies at the heart of the human experience. When we come to the end of our resources—in life or in death—and find them wanting, we are completely and totally dependent for our well-being, our vitality, our wholeness, and our sense of identity upon the mercy and kindness of God—in short, upon God's grace.

Pilgrims along life's way have experienced God's grace as making the difference between knowing where you are and being "lost"; between hope and despair; between seeing and being blind; between the miry clay and solid ground. God's grace makes the difference between the depths of what might have been and the heights of what will be. It is the divine ingredient in any situation that can transform defeat into victory, loss into gain, and death into life. Grace has brought the pilgrim safely through life's "many dangers, toils, and snares" and most certainly, with the crossing of the River, will bring the pilgrim home. Grace is the bridge to eternal life.

Chapter 6

Home

Surely goodness and mercy shall follow me
    all the days of my life;
and I shall dwell in the house of the LORD
    for ever.
(Ps. 23:6, RSV)

Lord, thou hast been our dwelling place in all generations. (Ps. 90:1, KJV)

These all died in faith, not having received what was
promised, but having seen it and greeted it from afar,
and having acknowledged that they were strangers
and exiles on the earth. For people who speak thus
make it clear that they are seeking a homeland. . . .
[T]hey desire a better country, that is, a heavenly
one. Therefore God is not ashamed to be called their
God, for he has prepared for them a city. (Heb.
11:13–16, RSV)

Jesus answered him, "If a man loves me, he will keep
my word, and my Father will love him, and we will
come to him and make our home with him." (John
14:23, RSV)

. . . and I heard a loud voice from the throne saying,
"Behold, the dwelling of God is with men. He will
dwell with them, and they shall be his people, and
God himself will be with them. . . . (Rev. 21:3, RSV)

• • •

To an open house in the evening
Home shall men come,
To an older place than Eden
And a taller town than Rome.
To the end of the way of the wandering star,
To the things that cannot be and that are,
To the place where God was homeless
And all men are at home.
        (Gilbert K. Chesterton, 1874–1936)

Song of the Road Home

The white cloud knows its way back
To the shadow of the hill,
The weary bird knows its path home
To the forest on the hill,
The sun knows where to sink back
Down in the distant ocean waters,
I alone am restless
In the distant wilderness.

The traveling child returns home,
Back to the Father's embrace.
Peacefully resting in You,
Could the child bear to leave again?
You, the dwelling place throughout
All generations, our eternal home. . . .
            (Weifan Wang, translated by
            Kim-kwang Chan, 1997.
            Based on sacred music of
            the Ming Dynasty)

Swing low, sweet chariot,
Comin' for to carry me home,
Swing low, sweet chariot,
Comin' for to carry me home.
            (African Spiritual)

Our God our Help in ages past,
Our Hope for years to come,
Our Shelter from the stormy blast,
And our eternal Home.

(Isaac Watts, 1719)

• • •

Of all the words in the English language, the one preferred for describing "heaven" is the word "home." "Home" is where I feel most comfortable, where I am surrounded by familiar things and with my family. It is where I no longer have to pretend, where I can "let my hair down" and relax. It is where I feel secure, at ease, and "at home."

Strange that such a word is the word of choice for describing how we feel about a place we have never been! Yet, instinctively from feelings deep within, we speak of the "heavenly home" as a place we have known from the beginning. Heaven is like the enchanted place of childhood memories where things are the way they always should be. Heaven is not some bizarre place beyond the farthest galaxy, which can only be reached by a time capsule or spaceship as in some science-fiction novel. Heaven is more like the familiar haunts of the good old days when all the family was together.

Yet real homes here on earth never quite live up to our ideal images. Earthly homes, even at their best, fall short of what we would like to remember. And at their worst, they can be wretched places indeed. To speak of heaven as home is to acknowledge that here we are pilgrims and strangers without any permanent abiding place.

Deep within our souls the image of the heavenly home has molded the memory of the earthly home. The heavenly home is the reality, the earthly home the pale substitute. The heavenly home is the ideal from which the image of our imperfect earthly home is derived.

Central to the memory of "home" are the parents. Stephen Foster's plaintive melody speaks of "the old folks at home." Home is to be in the "Father's house." Without "the Father," the image of "home" is an empty facade. Being "at home" means that God's dwelling is once more, as it was in the beginning, with God's children.

Chapter 7

"Well Done"

"*N*ow after a long time the master of those servants came and settled accounts with them. . . . And he also who had the two talents came forward, saying, 'Master, you delivered to me two talents; here I have made two talents more.' His master said to him, 'Well done, good and faithful servant; you have been faithful over a little, I will set you over much; enter into the joy of your master.'" (Matt. 25:19–23, RSV)

"When the Son of man comes in his glory, and all the angels with him, then he will sit on his glorious throne. . . . Then the King will say to those at his right hand, 'Come, O blessed of my Father, inherit the kingdom prepared for you from the foundation of the world; for I was hungry and you gave me food, I was thirsty and you gave me drink, I was a stranger and you welcomed me, I was naked and you clothed me, I was sick and you visited me, I was in prison and you came to me.' Then the righteous will answer him, 'Lord, when did we see thee hungry and feed thee, or thirsty and give thee drink? And when did we see thee a stranger and welcome thee, or naked and clothe thee? And when did we see thee sick or in prison and visit thee?' And the King will answer them, 'Truly, I say to you, as you did it to one of the least of these my brethren, you did it to me." (Matt. 25:31–40, RSV)

• • •

Then I saw in my dream that these two men [Hopeful and Christian] went in at the Gate, and lo, as they entered, they were transfigured. . . . Then I heard in my Dreams that all the Bells in the City rang again for joy, and that it was said unto them, "Enter ye into the joy of your Lord. . . ." (John Bunyan, *Pilgrim's Progress,* 154)

> Servant of God, well done!
> Rest from thy loved employ:
> The battle fought, the victory won,
> Enter thy Master's joy.
>
> The pains of death are past,
> Labour and sorrow cease,
> And Life's long warfare closed at last,
> Thy soul is found in peace.
>   (James Montgomery, 1771–1854)

• • •

The first word the servant hears is a word of commendation: "Well done." The first words spoken by the King on his glorious throne are ones of approval: "Come, O blessed of my Father, inherit the kingdom prepared for you. . . ." The first word the pilgrim hears is a word of welcome. Other words will surely follow, for there are corrections to be made, rebukes spoken, and new assignments given. But for a beginning this much is enough: "Well done."

The two-talent servant receives the same words of commendation as the five-talent servant, but each is given different responsibilities in keeping with their ability. Only the one-talent servant, who didn't even try, receives nothing.

The words of commendation come as a surprise. They are spoken in regard to acts done when no one was watching. We are quick to ask: "But Lord, what about the times I denied you? What about the times I miserably failed? What about the many opportunities I missed?" To each question the response is the same: "Well done. I was there. I was watching. I understood."

The words of commendation are not spoken in regard to religious acts of devotion. They are not spoken in regard to acts of heroism or courage. Some are spoken in regard to simple, ordinary deeds faithfully done in the performance of one's daily duty. Others are spoken in regard to random acts of mercy for the least of those in the human family: giving food or drink to those who were starving, providing clothes and shelter for those who were freezing, caring for those wasting away from disease, and visiting those who were locked up in some foul prison cell. Who are these nameless ones? We are not told. Yet they would certainly include the widows of Kosovo, the street children of São Paulo, the refugees of the Sudan, and the homeless people of Atlanta. Jesus Christ interposes himself between the Christian and the stranger in need. When you deal with the stranger, you are dealing with Jesus Christ: "In as much as you have done it unto the least of these my brothers or sisters you did it unto me."

Chapter 8

A Place Prepared

. . . *f*or I am going there on purpose to prepare a place for you. And if I go and prepare a place for you, I shall come again and receive you to myself, so that where I am you may be also. (John 14:2–3, NEB)

Come, O blessed of my Father, inherit the kingdom prepared for you from the foundation of the world. . . . (Matt. 25:34, RSV)

• • •

Your place in heaven will seem to be made for you and you alone, because you were made for it, made for it stitch by stitch as a glove is made for a hand. (C. S. Lewis, *The Problem of Pain*, 135–36)

Heaven is a prepared place for a prepared people. The word "heaven" speaks of home, the home of God and his people. . . . Heaven is a place of welcome. Jesus is waiting to say, "Come on in; I have a place prepared for you. God never takes his people to an unprepared place. . . ." (M. Chandrakumar, *Decision Magazine*)

Jesus said: "Where I am, there you will also be." For the Christian, heaven is where Jesus is. We do not need to speculate on what heaven will be like. It is enough to know that we will be forever with Him. (William Barclay, *The Gospel of John*, vol. 2, 181)

. . . and then what will all earthly joys be, compared to the promise: "Where I am, there ye may be also (John 14:3)." (Dag Hammarskjöld, *Markings,* 37)

• • •

When pilgrims arrive after weary travel, each will find a special, prepared place. The Host stands at the open door and speaks to each guest: "Welcome home. I have just the place for you. It has your name written on it. It's all 'made up.' It will fit you to a T."

Each pilgrim is a unique human being. Each is created in the image of God but is like none of God's other creatures. Each has special needs, special characteristics, special talents, and special contributions to make. Each will bring to the Father's house, gifts that no other pilgrim can bring. And so each has a place designed to suit one's individual personality.

Nothing in heaven is mass-produced. Nothing comes off the assembly line. The citizens of heaven are not clones or robots to be assigned to monotonous rows of look-alike cubbyholes. Each place will be tailor-made. "One size fits all" does not apply to heaven.

Heaven's preparation has not been haphazard. It has been going on for a long time, since the "foundation of the world." The preparation will include bits and pieces from our earthly pilgrimage. Somehow, circumstances and bitter ordeals that have not made any sense will be woven into the fabric of the grand design to add brilliant colors and rare beauty to the tapestry of eternal life.

A place prepared! So much we do not know and that does not concern me. But this much is clear: All the preparations that are being made have but one purpose. The one making the arrangements, The Lord of Life—the Stranger of Galilee who walked these same earthly paths so many years ago and who knows us better than we know ourselves—wants us to have a place nearby so that we might be forever with the Lord.

Chapter 9

Many Mansions

*L*et not your heart be troubled: ye believe in God, believe also in me. In my Father's house are many mansions (Greek: *monai*): if it were not so, I would have told you. (John 14:1–2, KJV)

If a man love me, he will keep my words: and my Father will love him, and we will come unto him, and make our abode (Greek: *monai*) with him. (John 14:23, KJV)

He came to his own home, and his own people received him not. (John 1:11, RSV)

"Foxes have holes, and birds of the air have nests; but the Son of man has nowhere to lay his head." (Matt 8:20, RSV)

• • •

Creation of Heaven

King, you created heaven according to your delight,
A place that is safe and pure,
Its air filled with the songs of angels. . . .

It is like an open meadow, in which all can move
    freely,
With people arriving from earth but never leaving.

It is huge, ten times the size of earth, so that every
    creature ever born can find a place.

It is small, no bigger than a village
Where all are friends and none is a stranger.

In the center is a palace, its walls made of emerald,
And its gates of amethyst, and on each gate is hung
A golden cross. . . .

Round the lawn walks a King, not dressed in fine robes,
But in a simple white tunic, smiling and embracing
Those he meets. . . .

Everyone in heaven is free to come to the palace,
And then to take with them its perfect peaceful joy; and
    in this way
The whole of Heaven is infused with the joy of the
    palace.

(From *The Celtic Psalter, c. 800 A.D.*)

• • •

The King James Version of the Bible speaks of the "many mansions" in the Father's house. It is a beautiful translation that has captured the imagination of English-language readers. But "mansion" brings to mind the lordly estates of the wealthy. The Revised Standard Version calls it "rooms." But "rooms" is too restricted, and confining. Perhaps "dwellings" or "abiding places" makes for a better translation.

The Greek word *monai* appears only twice in the New Testament, both times in this chapter. "The word seems to be deliberately chosen to express the fact that our earthly state is transitory and provisional compared with eternal and blessed being with God" (Gerhard Kittel, *Theological Dictionary of the New Testament,* vol. 4, 580). The permanence, indestructibility, and spaciousness of the dwelling place is emphasized here. There is ample room for all. Each pilgrim will have room to spread out. No one need feel crowded. Space is needed for each to be oneself. It will be a "cozy" place of warmth and intimacy but with the freedom to move about, to explore new territory, to experience both solitude and friendship—all within the overarching unity of "the Father's House."

In the first use of *monai* in this chapter, Christ is preparing the "abode" in heaven for his disciples. In the second use of the term, the disciples prepare their hearts as an "abode" on earth for the Lord. But it is not simply preparing a place "for the Lord," because the Lord belongs to a great multitude of people who have no abiding place.

Contrast the spaciousness of the heavenly habitat with the homelessness of millions here on earth. Think of those living in hovels on the garbage dumps of Cairo, the boat people of Hong Kong, the barrios of Latin America, the congested cities of Asia, and the slums of North America. One hundred million children live not in "abiding places" but on the streets of the world's cities.

Can we speak of the homelessness of God? The Christ came to "his own home, and his own people received him not" (John 1:11, RSV). The Son of man, who had had nowhere to lay his head, shared the experience of the world's homeless people. The spaciousness of heaven and the vision of the Christ alone on our streets call out for us to make room for all.

Chapter 10

"Remember Me"

*O*ne of the criminals who were hanged there kept deriding him. . . . But the other rebuked him, saying, "Do you not fear God, since you are under the same sentence of condemnation? . . . Then he said, "Jesus, remember me when you come into your kingdom." He (Jesus) replied, "Truly, I tell you, today you will be with me in Paradise." (Luke 23:39–43, NRSV)

He said to them, "I have eagerly desired to eat this Passover with you before I suffer. . . ." Then he (Jesus) took a loaf of bread, and when he had given thanks, he broke it and gave it to them (the disciples) saying, "This is my body, which is given for you. Do this in remembrance of me." (Luke 22:15–20, NRSV)

"Are not five sparrows sold for two pennies? Yet not one of them is forgotten in God's sight. . . . You are of more value than many sparrows." (Luke 12:6–7, NRSV)

• • •

Alzheimer's disease . . . robs the sufferer not only of the present and future but also of the past as all memory of prior events, relationships, and persons slips away. . . . Memory is what makes our lives. Life without memory is no life at all. . . . Our memory is our coherence, our reason, our feeling, even our action. Without it we are nothing. . . . Caregivers can be not only givers of care but bestowers of a kind of immortality by recalling for others around them what the person with Alzheimer's disease no longer can recall in order to strengthen the remembering of that person and to keep his or her role in the community alive in the corporate memory. . . . It is also possible to speak of God's memory in this light. Whether the individual remembers, or even whether the community remembers for the individual, the Western religious tradition certainly affirms that God remembers. Some comfort, therefore, can be found in the fact that God's memory is unfailing, even if that of any given human being is defective or even totally lost. God never forgets. (Stephen Sapp, "Living with Alzheimer's: Body, Soul, and the Remembering Community")

• • •

Two very different men who were facing death asked for the same thing. They wanted to be remembered. The criminal on the cross asked of Jesus, "Remember me when you come into your kingdom." Jesus Christ, when he was eating his last meal with his friends, asked that they remember him: "Do this in remembrance of me."

To be remembered is a universal desire. To be remembered, people have built pyramids, erected monuments, written books, and carved names and places in stone.

The criminal had no reason to think that anyone would want to remember him. Certainly, he had no claim on the memory of the unknown fellow sufferer whom he had scarcely met. He had done nothing noteworthy to warrant being remembered. Yet Jesus responded instantly to his request. Because Jesus remembered him, the criminal will be remembered by the world forever. If Jesus would remember such a person, how could he possibly forget you or me if we ask him to remember? *You will be remembered!*

Think of the pathos of that scene in the upper room. Jesus

asked but for one thing—to be remembered! How could his disciples forget him? Could they forget the one who had shared with them the Father's glory and with whom they had walked and talked and broken bread together for three years? And yet they did. The poignant words spoken at the Last Supper gave them a simple deed to prod their memory: "Do this in remembrance of me."

Jesus was also concerned that those who would follow the first-century disciples would forget. We say we will never forget, and yet we do. We forget loved ones and friends of long ago. We have a hard time remembering names, anniversaries, shopping lists, and even the Lord of Glory.

Memory is a precious, fragile commodity that we seek desperately to hold on to and yet which keeps slipping away. The demons of Alzheimer's may try to strip us and those we love of all memory and meaning. But these words of Jesus on the cross and at the Table speak the last word to the victims of Alzheimer's and their caretakers. Jesus remembers and wants us to remember! If our memories are with Jesus, they will endure forever.

Some time ago I was struggling to make sense of a new computer. Suddenly the computer screen went blank. A document that was of some importance to me had disappeared, vanished into thin air. None of the buttons that I pressed brought it back. In great distress I phoned my computer "guru" and called for help. "Don't touch a thing," he said, "I will be right over." In a few minutes the problem was diagnosed, and the document was back on the screen. To use a good computer term that is also good theology, the work had been "saved." Deep within the consciousness of the hard disk the words had been preserved. Not one line or one word was missing. Even the typos were all there!

Here is a parable of life. Yes, my memory may be slipping. And, yes, the demons of Alzheimer's have robbed the memories of some of those I love. But the words Jesus spoke on the cross and at the Table speak a word of hope to the victims of this dread disease, to those who have lost loved ones to its ravages, and to caregivers who struggle daily to bring what comfort they can. We can shout back in defiance to the demons of Alzheimer's:

> You can't have my memory. And you cannot take away the memory of those I love. You may think you have destroyed it. But you haven't. True, for a short time you may have it within your grasp. But I have committed to Jesus Christ my memory and the memory of my loved ones whom you are tormenting. He has "saved" it in the computer banks of heaven. It is beyond your reach. And in God's own time, it will be "downloaded" again into human consciousness. And not one thought or word or person or event will be forgotten.

Until that time comes, we gather around the Table of Memory. Here the community of faith embraces those who, for a little while, have lost the way. The community remembers what individuals can no longer recall. Here at the Table we remember and are remembered.

Chapter 11

Paradise

*O*ne of the criminals hanging there hurled insults at him: "Aren't you the Messiah? Save yourself and us!" The other one, however, rebuked him, saying, "Don't you fear God? You received the same sentence he did. Ours, however, is only right, because we are getting what we deserve for what we did; but he has done no wrong." And he said to Jesus, "Remember me, Jesus, when you come as King!" Jesus said to him, "I promise you that today you will be in Paradise with me." (Luke 23:39–43, TEV)

"To everyone who conquers, I will give permission to eat from the tree of life that is in the paradise of God." (Rev. 2:7, NRSV)

• • •

The answer of Jesus . . . goes beyond what is asked, for it promises the thief that already to-day he will enjoy fellowship with Jesus in Paradise. . . . Paradise is opened even to the irredeemably lost man hanging on the cross. He is promised fellowship with the Messiah. This shows how unlimited is the remission of sins in the age of forgiveness which has now dawned. (Gerhard Kittel, *Theological Dictionary of the New Testament,* V, 765–70)

If God hath made this world so fair,
Where sin and death abound,
How beautiful beyond compare,
Will paradise be found!
(James Montgomery, 1771–1854)

• • •

"Paradise" is a rare word found only three times in the New Testament. Paul uses it to describe what cannot be described when he recalls his mystical vision of highest heaven (2 Cor. 12:4). In the book of Revelation, "Paradise" is identified with the Garden of Eden, which is reopened, and those who have conquered will be given permission to eat of the fruit of the tree of life (Rev. 2:7). Jesus chooses this exotic word when he responds to the request of his tormented fellow sufferer.

Paradeisos is a "loan word" from the Persian and refers to the lush, green garden of a king or nobleman. The word brings to mind a pavilion, fruit trees, shade, and running water. Outside the high wall of the garden the heat of the desert might be stifling, but inside all is serene, peaceful, and cool. It is an oasis in the desert.

What better word could Jesus have chosen to bring relief to a sufferer on the cross who was dying of thirst! Jesus' response was instant. There was no hesitation. No time for delay: "Today you shall be with me in Paradise." Relief is on the way: Think of flowing streams of water, juicy fruit from bountiful trees, cool shade, and a refreshing breeze. Not in the distant future but "today."

The response goes far beyond what had been requested. The criminal had only asked for "remembrance." Jesus extends an invitation to this lonely man to share companionship in "paradise." Whatever his past, the criminal is forgiven, accepted, and restored. One might have thought that such a person who had not demonstrated any of the Christian virtues during his life would have been assigned space on the outer fringes of heaven. But, no, he is brought to the very center to enjoy fellowship with the Christ in the Paradise of God.

With these words to the criminal who had been sentenced to die, Jesus identifies himself with all those on death row. Whether innocent or guilty is hardly the question; Jesus is there with them. Jesus puts himself in the position of those being tortured by secret police or depraved serial killers. He identifies with those who are held hostage by terrorist gangs in foreign lands who do not know whether they will live or die. His words speak to those who are wracked with the pain of disease and all those who face the extremities of life— alone. Jesus was there. Jesus remembers. The pain will stop, sooner rather than later. The garden of God is waiting.

Chapter 12

The Body

Some Sadducees, who say there is no resurrection, came to him and asked him a question. . . . Jesus said to them, "Is not this the reason you are wrong, that you know neither the scriptures nor the power of God?. . . And as for the dead being raised, have you not read in the book of Moses, in the story about the bush, how God said to him, 'I am the God of Abraham, the God of Isaac, and the God of Jacob'? He is God not of the dead, but of the living; you are quite wrong." (Mark 12:18–27, NRSV)

But someone will ask, "How are the dead raised? With what kind of body do they come?" . . . What you sow does not come to life unless it dies. And as for what you sow, you do not sow the body that is to be, but a bare seed, perhaps of wheat or of some other grain. But God gives it a body as he has chosen, and to each kind of seed its own body. Not all flesh is alike, but there is one flesh for human beings, another for animals, another for birds, and another for fish. There are both heavenly bodies and earthly bodies. . . . There is one glory of the sun, and another glory of the moon, and another glory of the stars; indeed, star differs from star in glory.

So it is with the resurrection of the dead. What is sown is perishable, what is raised is imperishable. It is sown in dishonor, it is raised in glory. It is sown in weakness, it is raised in power. It is sown a physical body, it is raised a spiritual body. (1 Cor. 15:35–44, NRSV)

• • •

I believe in . . . the resurrection of the body and the life everlasting. . . . (Apostles' Creed, 710–24 A.D.)

Question: "What benefits do believers receive from Christ at death?"
Answer: "The souls of believers are at their death made perfect in holiness, and do immediately pass into glory, and their bodies, being still united to Christ, do rest in their graves till the resurrection." (*Shorter Catechism,* 1646 A.D.)

Do you want to believe in the living Christ? We may believe in him only if we believe in his corporeal resurrection. This is the content of the New Testament. We are always free to reject it, but not to modify it, nor to pretend that the New Testament tells something else. We may accept or refuse the message, but we may not change it. . . . What is the meaning of the Christian hope in this life? A life after death? A tiny soul which like a butterfly flutters away above the grave and is still preserved somewhere, in order to live on immortally? That is not the Christian hope. "I believe in the resurrection of the body." Body in the Bible is quite simply man, man, moreover under the sign of sin. And to this man it is said, Thou shall rise again. Resurrection means not the continuation of life, but life's completion. . . . The Christian hope does not lead us away from this life. It is the conquest of death, not a flight into the Beyond. (Karl Barth, interview with the editors of *Time* magazine, April 20, 1962.)

It is at this point that awe and trembling fall upon us as we read the records. If the story is false, it is at least a much stranger story than we expected. . . If the story is true, then a wholly new mode of being has arisen in the universe. . .

The record represents Christ as passing after death (as no one has passed before) neither into a purely . . . "spiritual" mode of existence nor into a "natural" life such as we know, but into a life which has its own, new Nature. . . . The picture is not what we expected. . . . It is not the picture of an escape from any and every kind of Nature into some unconditional and utterly transcendent life. It is the picture of a new human nature, and a new Nature in general, being brought into existence. . . . This is the picture— not of unmaking but of remaking. The old field of space, time, matter, and the senses is to be weeded, dug, and sown for a new crop. (C. S. Lewis, *Miracles*, 176–79)

If God cannot redeem the body that is so central to personal integrity, then God's victory over death is partial and relatively feeble. Resurrection and divine power are indissolubly linked. (Kyle A. Pasewark, *The Christian Century,* April 10, 1996)

Everything that is bound up with a person's name—everything that the name means is "preserved" in the resurrection and transformed: "I have redeemed you. I have called you by name. You are mine" (Isaiah 43:1). What is meant here is not the soul, a "kernel" of the person's existence, or some inward point of identity but the whole configuration of the person's life, the whole life history and all the conditions that are meant by his or her name. (Jurgen Moltmann, *The Coming of God,* 75)

• • •

The questions asked by the Corinthian Christians of the apostle Paul are very relevant today. In the face of the disintegration of our bodies and the decomposition of flesh and blood, how can we think of anyone being "raised from the dead"? Today it may be the vogue to think of disembodied souls or of vague, benign spirits that escape from bondage to their earthly bodies to continue some kind of forlorn and lonely existence beyond the clouds and the pearly gates. Could life after death be compared to a drop of water returning to the ocean from which it came? Or possibly it is conceived of as an escape from the wheel of life to the emptiness of "Nirvana," or maybe as the transmigration of souls through an endless procession of life forms.

These are *not* the view of the Christian faith. From the earliest days, Christians of all theological persuasions—Roman Catholics, Orthodox, and Protestants—have insisted that the New Testament bears witness to a resurrection of a reunited spirit *and* body beyond the grave. The New Testament meets head-on the challenge of death. No halfway answers will do. The "sting" of death is removed (1 Cor. 15:55). Death has been "swallowed up" in victory (1 Cor. 15:54). Death has simply been "abolished" (2 Tim. 1:10). This "last enemy" of humanity will be destroyed (1 Cor. 15:26). Death will be "no more" (Rev. 21:4).

This is the meaning of the "resurrection of the body." It affirms the total survival of the whole personality. The "body" is that which defines my individuality. To sever soul from body results in a truncated, deformed entity that falls far short of the goal of human destiny to which the Scriptures point. What kind of heaven would it be if it was a kingdom where God presided over an assembly of robots, clones, or zombies?

To make this point Jesus reaches back to the most ancient traditions of the Jewish Scriptures. Moses stands before the burning bush. God introduces himself in these words: "I am the God of your fathers, the God of Abraham, the God of Isaac, and the God of Jacob." God is not the God of the dead but of the living—living people, individuals, and personalities!

The body that is "raised" will certainly be different from the body that is laid to rest in the ground. The difference is difficult for us to comprehend, but Paul's analogy of the different kinds of "body" (animal, human, celestial) may help.

Each has it own distinct characteristics. Each has its own defining "glory." The glory of heaven lies in the incredible diversity of its inhabitants. Heaven will be teeming with the variety and vitality of its citizens. Each will have its own "body" with its own distinct personality. Each will have a mission to fulfill. Each will bear its own distinct fruit.

Jesus, in defining his own death and resurrection, told the parable of the seed that fell into the ground and died. The differences between the seed that is sown and the plant that came up are obvious, and yet the continuity between the two is unmistakable. The fully grown plant is the same species as the seed that was sown. The plant is not *less* but *more* than the seed from which it had sprung.

What assurances do we have for all of this? The Christian Church has staked its claim of truth on one event: the resurrection of Jesus Christ. The tomb was empty. Christ was raised from the dead on the third day. He appeared to the twelve and to five hundred brothers and sisters in the faith. As our forerunner, he has penetrated the veil of death and will return to prepare the way for his believers. In due time, the one who raised Christ from the dead will give life to our mortal bodies.

Chapter 13

Clean

> *W*ash yourselves; make yourselves clean. . . ;
> Cease to do evil,
>   learn to do good;
> seek justice,
>   correct oppression;
> defend the fatherless,
>   plead for the widow. . . .
> Though your sins are like scarlet,
>   they shall be as white as snow;
> though they be red like crimson,
>   they shall become like wool.
> (Isa. 1:16–18, RSV)

> Wash me thoroughly from my iniquity,
>   And cleanse me from my sin. . . .
> Purge me with hyssop, and I shall be clean;
>   wash me, and I shall be whiter than snow.
> (Ps. 51:2, 7, NRSV)

> . . . O Jerusalem!
> How long will it be
> before you are made clean?
> (Jer. 13:27, NRSV)

After this I looked, and behold, a great multitude . . .
standing before the throne and before the Lamb,
clothed in white robes. . . . Then one of the elders
addressed me, saying, "Who are these, clothed in

white robes, and whence have they come?" I said to him,
"Sir, you know." And he said to me, "These are they who
have . . . washed their robes and made them white in the
blood of the Lamb." (Rev. 7:9–14, RSV)

But nothing unclean shall enter it [the city], nor any one
who practices abomination or falsehood, but only those who
are written in the Lamb's book of life. (Rev. 21:27, RSV)

• • •

Wash, Lord, and purify my heart,
And make it clean in every part;
And when tis clean, Lord, keep it too,
For that is more than I can do.
(Thomas Elwood in R. E. Speer's
Five Minutes a Day, 145)

• • •

Would you rather be clean or dirty? If you are a human
being then you would rather be clean. In one of the fantasies
of C. S. Lewis, a pilgrim, foul and filthy from his travels,
arrives at the gate of heaven. Would we not be shocked and
disappointed, says Lewis, if God welcomed the new arrival
with these words: "It is true my son that your breath smells
and your rags drip with mud and slime, but we are charitable
here and no one will upbraid you with these things, nor draw
away from you. Enter into the joy of your Lord." Would we
not then want our pilgrim to reply: "With submission, Sir,
and if there is no objection, I'd rather be cleansed first." And
to the warning, "It may hurt, you know," we would have our
pilgrim reply, "Even so, Sir, make me clean" (C. S. Lewis,
Letters to Malcolm, 108–9).

The prophets of the Old Testament were obsessed with the
problem of cleanliness. It began with ceremonial cleanliness
in the book of Leviticus but more and more the emphasis

became one of cleanliness of bodies, minds, and hearts—of thoughts, deeds, and desires. God was holy, and the first requirement for those who would stand in his presence was to have "clean hands and pure hearts" (Ps. 24:4, NRSV). The ideal of a holy nation dwelling in a clean environment was never fully realized by the prophets, but they looked forward to its fulfillment in the Messianic age.

And so it should come as no surprise that cleanliness is one of the characteristics of the New Jerusalem. One of the first impressions of the city would be the spectacular array of a great multitude dressed in dazzling white robes.

Robes! They are garments of dignity and honor. Important people wore robes. Each was the same, without insignia or rank, the same for men or women. White robes signified the new life in Jesus Christ. Each robe may have at one time been soiled, even filthy, but no more. Each pilgrim had taken care to do his or her own laundry. The pilgrims had washed their own robes until they were brilliantly clean and spotless.

Each had been washed in the "blood of the lamb." The image is powerful but for us too vivid and perhaps even repulsive. What does it mean? Think of the first Passover in Egypt when the blood of the lamb sprinkled on the doorpost brought deliverance. Think of the long, unbroken line of animal sacrifices that for over one thousand years had been offered up each day in tabernacle and temple. Think of the communion table and the blood of the covenant poured out for the forgiveness of sins. Think of the Lamb on the throne "slain from the foundation of the world" (Rev. 13:8, KJV). Think of the martyred saints who had washed their robes and made them white in the "blood of the lamb." A mystery? Yes, but all the images point to the truth that cleanliness has its price. Cleanliness is a communal affair, and one of the characteristics of the city is its strict environmental controls. "Nothing unclean" is given permission to enter. The planners of the city insist on clean streets, clean air, clean water, clean clothes, clean people, and clean hearts.

Today we are discovering anew the fact that the city which wants to be clean cannot tolerate individuals who would flaunt the public welfare by dumping garbage on the streets or polluting water and air with foul refuse. For a sustainable society in the next millennium, even stricter controls over environmental hazards and nuclear waste will be necessary. Would that our society today had the same intolerance for the moral pollution of Hollywood, Radio City, and Madison Avenue as it has for acid rain, landfills, and smog.

Chapter 14

Rest

*G*od saw everything that he had made, and indeed, it was very good. . . . Thus the heavens and the earth were finished, and all their multitude. And on the seventh day God finished the work that he had done, and he rested on the seventh day from all the work that he had done. So God blessed the seventh day and hallowed it, because on it God rested from all the work that he had done in creation. (Gen. 1:31–2:3, NRSV)

Remember the Sabbath day to keep it holy. Six days you shall labor and do all your work, but the seventh day is a Sabbath to the LORD your God. (Ex. 20:8–10, RSV)

Come to me, all you that are weary and are carrying heavy burdens, and I will give you rest. Take my yoke upon you, and learn from me; for I am gentle and humble in heart, and you will find rest for your souls. (Matt. 11:28–29, NRSV)

So then, a sabbath rest still remains for the people of God; for those who enter God's rest also cease from their labors as God did from his. Let us therefore make every effort to enter that rest. . . . (Heb. 4:9–11, NRSV)

And I heard a voice from heaven saying, ". . . Blessed are the dead who from now on die in the

Lord," "Yes," says the Spirit, "they will rest from their labors, for their deeds follow them." (Rev. 14:13, NRSV)

• • •

There's a fancy some lean to and others hate
    That, when this life is ended begins
New work for the soul in another state,
    Where it strives and gets weary, loses and wins:
Where the strong and the weak, this world's congeries,
    Repeat in large what they practiced in small
Through life after life in unlimited series,
    Only the scale's to be changed, that's all.

Yet I hardly know. When a soul has seen
    By the means of Evil that God is best,
And through earth and its noise what is heaven's serene—
    When our faith in the same has stood the test—
When the child turned man, you burn the rod,
    The uses of labor are surely done,
There remaineth a rest for the people of God:
    And I have had trouble enough, for one.
                    (Robert Browning, 1812–1889)

        New graces ever gaining
        From this our day of rest,
        We reach the rest remaining
        To spirits of the blest.
        To Holy Ghost be praises,
        To Father and to Son;
        The Church her voice upraises
        To Thee, blest Three in One.
            (Christopher Wordsworth, 1862)

    O Sabbath rest by Galilee,
    O calm of hills above,
    Where Jesus knelt to share with thee
    The silence of eternity,
        Interpreted by love!

Drop Thy still dews of quietness,
in all our strivings cease;
Take from our souls the strain and stress,
And let our ordered lives confess
The beauty of Thy peace.
(John Greenleaf Whittier, 1872)

Day of all the week the best,
Emblem of eternal rest . . .
(John Newton, 1774)

• • •

The harmony of work and rest is imbedded in the very
framework of creation. The health of our bodies, minds, and
souls depends upon the interplay of intense activity followed
by periods of quietness. Rest provides time for healing. It
offers the opportunity for contemplation as to the meaning of
what lies behind and preparation for what lies ahead.

The Sabbath rest is one of the greatest gifts of the Jews. It
was the first great act of labor legislation and served to pro-
tect the toiling masses, slaves, working children, and even
the beasts of burden from the greed and avarice of slave masters and exploiting rulers. Setting aside one day of rest in
seven has now become a standard throughout the world.

But the Sabbath is more than labor legislation. Human
beings rest because God rested. Because rest is an activity of
God, it is holy. Something of a sacramental quality occurs in
resting because it is commanded by the God who also rests,
who welcomes the weary, and who takes the burdens of those
that are heavily laden.

Resting is more than idleness or inactivity. It is the celebration of work that has been completed. God looked out
upon the cosmos that he had made to see how it had turned
out. As an artist lays down his brush, contemplates his mas-
terpiece, and savors the moment of completion, so God sat

back, surveyed his work of creation, and pronounced it all "very good."

The benefits of the Sabbath are only partially realized in this life. The Sabbath is a symbol of the perfect rest that lies ahead. "There remaineth a rest for the people of God." That rest is all the sweeter because of the times of weariness, fatigue, and exhaustion.

When the earthly routine of work is over, then the pilgrims "rest from their labors and their works do follow them." There is continuity between the rest in heaven and the works done on earth. No deeds of kindness or mercy will be forgotten. No act of faith or devotion will have been in vain. Deeds done on earth will be woven into the tapestry of the new world. They will live on forever.

Chapter 15

Work

*C*ursed is the ground because of you; in toil you shall eat of it all the days of your life; thorns and thistles it shall bring forth for you. . . . By the sweat of your face you shall eat bread. . . . (The expulsion from the Garden of Eden, Gen. 3:17–19, NRSV)

And there shall be no more curse: but the throne of God and of the Lamb shall be in it; and his servants shall serve him. . . . (Rev. 22:3, KJV)

". . . Well done, good and trustworthy slave; you have been trustworthy in a few things, I will put you in charge of many things. . . ." (Matt. 25:21, NRSV)

Therefore are they before the throne of God, and serve him day and night. . . . (Rev. 7:15, KJV)

• • •

Pilgrims ask on entering the Heavenly City . . . "What must we do in this holy place?" To whom it was answered, You must there receive the comfort of all your toil. . . . There also you shall serve him [the Holy One] continually with praise, with shouting, and thanksgiving, whom you desired to serve in the World, though with much difficulty, because of the infirmity of your flesh. . . . You shall . . . ride . . . with the King of Glory . . . and when he shall sit upon the throne of Judgement, you shall sit by him, yea and when he shall pass sentence . . . you also shall have a voice in that Judgement. . . ." (John Bunyan, *Pilgrim's Progress*, 152–53)

Some object to the Christian doctrine of immortality on the ground that it puts too much emphasis on everlasting rest. Unfortunately, quite a few Christians still think of heaven as a place of complete inaction. Yet such a concept is far removed from true restfulness. . . . In the divine presence our highest glory will not be achieved in idleness, but in laboring for Him whose service is perfect freedom and perfect rest." (John Sutherland Bonnell, *I Believe in Immortality*, 70–72)

Activity is the prelude to rest; and peace and companionship with God do not exclude activity. In the future world man's purified powers and capacities will be expressed in fuller service, free from all the laborious elements that make work in this world so often a thing of toil and pain. One of the chief joys of heaven will be the joy of loving service. (Donald W. Richardson, *The Revelation of Jesus Christ*, 140)

> When Earth's last picture is painted,
>   And the tubes are twisted and dried,
> When the oldest colors have faded,
>   And the youngest critic has died,
> We shall rest, and faith, we shall need it—
>   Lie down for an aeon or two,
> Till the Master of All Good Workmen
>   Shall put us to work anew.
>
> And those that were good shall be happy:
>   They shall sit in a golden chair;
> They shall splash at a ten-league canvas
>   With brushes of comets' hair;
> They shall find real saints to draw from—
>   Magdalene, Peter, and Paul;

> They shall work for an age at a sitting,
>   And never be tired at all.
>
> And only the Master shall praise us,
>   And only the Master shall blame;
> And no one shall work for money,
>   And no one shall work for fame;
> But each for the joy of working,
>   And each, in his separate star,
> Shall draw the Thing as he sees It
>   For the God of Things as They Are!
>   (Rudyard Kipling, 1865–1936)

• • •

For theologians and biblical scholars who write commentaries on these verses, work is satisfying and pleasant. But for most of the peoples who have lived on our planet since Adam was expelled from the garden, work has been backbreaking toil. For countless millions, work has been oppressive, dehumanizing drudgery at the hands of slave masters, greedy employers, and oppressive economic systems. For these millions, the news that the burden of work will end is fantastic good news.

The good news is not only that there will be ample time for rest but that work has been freed from drudgery and exploitation. In heaven, work is not eliminated; it is redeemed. The whole creation had shared in the "curse" that followed the expulsion from the Garden of Eden. But in the new creation, the cosmos will be set free from this bondage. Nature will be fruitful and productive to a degree we can hardly imagine. Thorns and thistles, tsetse flies and boll weevils, locust and garden pests are no more. Work and rest are in harmony once again.

What kind of work? Some versions describe it as "worship." But surely "worship" (the way we think of it as sitting on church pews, listening to sermons, and taking part in the liturgy) is too confining. Heaven would hardly be heaven if it meant sitting in church all day and every day! Other versions use the term "service," which is a better description as it includes many other kinds of activity.

What kinds of activity? Our finite minds are limited by time and space and so have a hard time grasping this concept. But here and there in scripture are hints and clues. The faithful servant who had been faithful in small matters on earth is given larger responsibilities in the life hereafter (Matt. 25:21). Jesus speaks of his twelve disciples sitting "on twelve thrones judging the twelve tribes of Israel" (Matt. 19:28, NRSV). The redeemed will take part somehow in the administration of justice (1 Cor. 6:2).

Of this much we can be sure. Work in heaven will be uniquely suited to my talents and abilities. It will be work that I, only I, can do best. It will be to the glory and honor of God.

Chapter 16

Children

*H*e shall feed his flock like a shepherd; he shall gather the lambs with his arm, and carry them in his bosom, and shall gently lead those that are with young. (Isa. 40:11, KJV)

And all thy children shall be taught of the LORD; and great shall be the peace of thy children. (Isa. 54:13, KJV)

. . . and a little child shall lead them. (Isa. 11:6, KJV)

He called a child, whom he put among them, and said, "Truly I tell you, unless you change and become like children, you will never enter the kingdom of heaven. Whoever becomes humble like this child is the greatest in the kingdom of heaven. Whoever welcomes one such child in my name welcomes me." (Matt. 18:2–5, NRSV)

"Take care that you do not despise one of these little ones; for, I tell you, in heaven their angels continually see the face of my Father in heaven." (Matt. 18:10, NRSV)

"Let the little children come to me, and do not stop them; for it is to such as these that the kingdom of heaven belongs." (Matt. 19:14, NRSV)

• • •

Two Litanies

Softly rose the litany:
    "Suffer them to come to me;
These my Father's chosen be,
    All the little children."
Where the faithful knelt in prayer,
To their Father singing, there
Trembling on the scented air
    Voices of the children.

Where the wheels of traffic groaned,
Men of Mammon, high enthroned
Other litany intoned
    For the little children:
Fiercely swelling, loud and strong,
Raucous rang their savage song
Where the chaffering traders throng:
    "Suffer, little children!"

    "Little faces, pinched and old,
Little fingers blue with cold,
Little lives ground into gold—
    Suffer, little children!"
Clacking looms make quick reply,
Whirring wheels took up the cry,
Echoing back hell's litany:
    "Suffer, little children!"
                (George I. Knapp in R. E. Speer's
                Five Minutes a Day, 264)

From Heaven the speechless infants speak:
Weep not (they say), our mothers dear,
For swords nor sorrows come not here,
Now we are strong who were so weak
And all is ours we could not seek.

We bloom among the blooming flowers
We sing among the singing birds;
Wisdom we have who wanted words;

Here morning knows not evening hours
All's rainbow here without its showers.

And softer than our mother's breast,
And closer than our mother's arm,
Is here the love that keeps us warm
And broods above our happy nest.
Dear mothers, come, for heaven is best.
(Christina Rosetti, in R. E. Speer's
Five Minutes a Day, 31)

Around the throne of God in heaven
Thousands of children stand,
Children whose sins are all forgiv'n
A holy happy band, singing
"Glory, glory, glory be to God on High."
(Anne H. Shepherd, *Children's Hymn,* 1854)

DONALD

Son of Mark and Nettie Grier
November 30, 1908

"And the streets of the city shall be full
of girls and boys playing"

(Tombstone of Paul Donaldson, aged 5 years
who died of diphtheria at the mission compound
in Suchowfu, China)

• • •

Are there children in heaven? Of course. How do you know? What would a nice place like heaven be without children?

Children on earth have suffered enough by neglect, carelessness, and exploitation. The most severe warning and word of judgment Jesus ever spoke was to those who abused little children (Matt. 18:6). He reserves his greatest blessing for those who go out of their way to care for children (Matt. 18:4).

That Jesus gives heaven's priority to children is not

surprising. Heaven belongs to them (Matt. 19:14). The qual-
ities of children prepare one for entrance into the kingdom
(Matt. 18:3–4). Children constantly gaze into the face of God
the Father (Matt. 18:10). Children can understand the ways
of heaven better than adults. Adults want it all to be rational
and "scientific."

Heaven is for all the seasons of life. Why then should the
season of childhood be excluded? Children are important not
just for what they can become as adults, but they are important for what they are—as children. Children are attracted to
heaven because other children are there. For little children,
what a solemn, serious, uninteresting place heaven would be
if only adults lived there. Children offer a dimension to life
in community that only they can bring. They add a sense of
wonder, excitement, and playfulness. They keep adults from
taking themselves too seriously.

Do children "grow up" in heaven? Children, as well as
adults, will continue their growth as unique persons, each
made in the image of God. Children teach us things that are
too simple for the wise and sophisticated to understand.
Maybe in heaven we will all be more like children than like
"grown-ups."

Chapter 17

Friends

I do not call you servants any longer, because the servant does not know what the master is doing; but I have called you friends, because I have made known to you everything that I have heard from my Father. (John 15:15, NRSV)

But we do not want you to be uninformed, brothers and sisters, about those who have died, so that you may not grieve as others do who have no hope. For since we believe that Jesus died and rose again, even so, through Jesus, God will bring with him those who have died. . . . Therefore encourage one another with these words. (1 Thess. 4:13–14, 18, NRSV)

Blessed are those who mourn, for they shall be comforted. (Matt. 5:4, RSV)

• • •

There you shall enjoy your friends again, that are gone thither before you; and there you shall with joy receive even every one that follows into the holy place after you. . . . (Bunyan, *Pilgrim's Progress*, 152)

Fundamental to our belief in immortality is our hope of reunion with those who have gone before. Indeed, eternal life would be without its deepest joys if love were to be deprived of its dearest object. (Bonnell, *I Believe in Immortality*, 64)

He is not dead, this friend—not dead
But, in the path we mortals tread,
Got some few, trifling steps ahead,
   And nearer to the end,
So that you, too, once past this bend,
Shall meet again, as face to face, this friend
   You fancy dead.
                    (Robert Louis Stevenson in
            Masterpieces of Religious Verse, 587)

Now the laborer's task is o'er;
   Now the battle day is past;
Now upon the farthest shore
   Lands the voyager at last.
Father, in thy gracious keeping
Leave we now Thy servant sleeping. . . .

"Earth to earth, and dust to dust,"
   Calmly now the words we say;
Left behind, we wait in trust
   For the resurrection day.
Father, in Thy gracious keeping
Leave we now Thy servant sleeping.
                    (John Ellerton in R. E. Speer's
                  Five Minutes a Day, 206)

It seemeth such a little way to me
   Across to that strange country—the Beyond;
And yet not strange, for it has grown to be
   The home of those of whom I am most fond;
They make it seem familiar and most dear,
   As journeying friends bring distant regions near. . . .

And so for me there is no sting to death,
   And so the grave has lost its victory.
It is but crossing—with abated breath.
   And white, set face—a little strip of sea,
To find the loved ones waiting on the shore,
   More beautiful, more precious than before.
                    (E. W. Wilcox in R. E. Speer's
                  Five Minutes a Day, 229)

• • •

Friendship is alive and well in heaven because of our one great friend—Jesus. Our relationship to him defines our relationship to each other—both in this life and in the next. He has known the joys of having comrades on earth, and these he has called to be his friends—forever.

We are not God's toys or playthings. We are not pawns that can be sacrificed for an advantage to be gained in greater games or wars throughout the universe. I am his friend! Quite amazingly, God will enjoy my fellowship as much as I will enjoy his.

Jesus knew the joys of human friendships. He knows how important and how precious they are to us. It would simply be unthinkable that within the broad expanses of heaven, room would not exist for these ongoing, continuing relationships between loved ones that began here on earth.

Visions of what goes on in heaven from the book of Revelation—dimly perceived to be sure—are full of group activities, such as the interchange between the elders, living creatures, and the great multitude that no one can number. Heaven includes the singing of choirs, prayers in unison, conquering armies, antiphonal responses, and feasting at the marriage supper of the Lamb. All are group activities in which people do not act in solitary grandeur but interact with each other. This is what friendship is all about.

Chapter 18

Communion of the Saints

*T*herefore, since we are surrounded by so great a cloud of witnesses, let us also lay aside every weight, and sin which clings so closely, and let us run with perseverance the race that is set before us, looking to Jesus the pioneer and perfecter of our faith, who for the joy that was set before him endured the cross, despising the shame, and is seated at the right hand of the throne of God. (Heb. 12:1–2, RSV)

• • •

I believe in the communion of the saints. . . . (The Apostles' Creed)

Heaven is the community of those whom God loves and who love God. All retain their personal characters, but woven together in perfect charity, so that in God's generous embrace each person among the millions whom God loves loves each other person among the millions whom God loves. It is like a weaving in which each thread touches every other thread in a spark of loving light, so that the whole web shines like a field of stars. In heaven all see and observe their love and grace and peace spread out to everyone and through everyone so that the love of each is realized perfectly and extended totally to each and to all. (Jeffrey Burton Russell, *A History of Heaven*, 5–6)

For all the saints who from their labors rest,
Who Thee by faith before the world confessed,
Thy name, O Jesus, be forever blessed,
    Alleluia!

Thou wast their Rock, their Fortress and their Might;
Thou, Lord, their Captain in the well-fought fight;
Thou in the darkness drear, the one true Light.
    Allelulia!

O may Thy soldiers, faithful, true and bold,
Fight as the saints who nobly fought of old,
And win with them, the victor's crown of gold.
    Allelulia!

O blest communion, fellowship divine!
We feebly struggle; they in glory shine,
Yet all are one in Thee, for all are Thine.
    Alleluia!

And when the strife is fierce, the warfare long,
Steals on the ear the distant triumph song,
And hearts are brave again, and arms are strong.
    Alleluia!

                        (William Walsham How, 1864)

• • •

"Friendship" is not a strong enough word to describe the
bond that unites all those whom God has called and whom
God loves. The church has called this reality "the communion of the saints." It has been an article of faith and included
in the creeds of Christendom from the earlier times. This
communion unites those who are divided by time and space.
The bond transcends differences of race and culture, dogma
and history, language and world view. It spans the centuries
and the continents and is at home in each millennium.
Newcomers who are just starting out on their pilgrimage are
included as well as those for whom the pilgrimage has been

completed. In some mystical fashion the communion links the saints "above" with the saints "below."

The communion is most vividly expressed in the roll call of the heroes of faith in the eleventh chapter of Hebrews. Mentioned are those who stood at the very threshold of human history: Abel, Enoch, and Noah. A high point is reached with Abraham and Sarah, the patriarchs, and Moses. We can add to the roll call the apostles of the New Testament, the martyrs of the early church, and missionaries and pilgrims of our own day. All these heroes are united in their response to the call of faith, their pilgrimage in seeking a better land, and their loyalty to the one God and Father of us all.

Then in the amphitheater scene in Hebrews 12, we are introduced as members of the "team" of pilgrims now on earth who run their races before a great cloud of witnesses. These witnesses are no ordinary spectators. They are the heroes of faith that were listed in chapter 11. Their presence and support give renewed courage and endurance to those engaged in the races. "An athlete would strive with double effort if he knew that a stadium of famous Olympic athletes was watching him" (Barclay, *The Letter to the Hebrews,* 195–96).

As we run our races here on earth, some of us, for whatever reason, are alone for long hours during the day and longer hours at night. The pangs of loneliness can sap our courage, weaken our spiritual strength, embitter our personalities, and bring us to the threshold of despair. But we are not alone! Witnesses are watching. We are part of a glorious community that encompasses heaven and earth and reaches out to enfold us in its loving embrace. We live and we die as part of this communion of faith, hope, and love.

Chapter 19

Banquet

*H*o, everyone who thirsts,
  come to the waters;
and you that have no money,
  Come, buy and eat!
Come, buy wine and milk
  Without money and without price.
Why do you spend your money
    for that which is not bread,
  and your labor for that which
    does not satisfy?
Listen carefully to me, and eat what is good,
  and delight yourself in rich food.
                                    (Isa. 55:1–2, NRSV)

"Blessed are those who hunger and thirst for righteousness, for they will be filled." (Matt. 5:6, NRSV)

Once more Jesus spoke to them in parables, saying: "The kingdom of heaven may be compared to a king who gave a wedding banquet for his son. He sent his slaves to call those who had been invited to the wedding banquet, but they would not come. Again he sent other slaves, saying, 'Tell those who have been invited: Look, I have prepared my dinner, my oxen and my fat calves have been slaughtered, and everything is ready. . . .'" (Matt. 22:1–4, NRSV)

While they were eating, Jesus took a loaf of bread, and after blessing it he broke it, gave it to the disciples, and said, "Take, eat; this is my body." Then he took a cup, and after giving thanks he gave it to them, saying, "Drink from it, all of you; for this is my blood of the covenant, which is poured out for many for the forgiveness of sins. I tell you, I will never again drink of this fruit of the vine until that day when I drink it new with you in my Father's kingdom." (Matt. 26:26–29, NRSV)

"I tell you, many will come from east and west and will eat with Abraham and Isaac and Jacob in the kingdom of heaven. . . ." (Matt. 8:11, NRSV)

And the angel said to me, "Write this: Blessed are those who are invited to the marriage supper of the Lamb." (Rev. 19:9, NRSV)

> The Spirit and the bride say, "Come."
> And let everyone who hears say, "Come."
> And let everyone who is thirsty come.
> Let anyone who wishes take the water of life as a gift.
> (Rev. 22:17, NRSV)

• • •

> Here would I feed upon the bread of God,
> Here drink with Thee the royal wine of heaven,
> Here would I lay aside each earthly load,
> Here taste afresh the calm of sin forgiven.

> This is the hour of banquet and of song,
> This is the heavenly Table spread for me:
> Here let me feast, and feasting, still prolong
> The brief, bright hour of fellowship with Thee.
> (Horatius Bonar, 1855)

> I should like a great lake of finest ale
> For the King of kings.
> I should like a table of the choicest food
> For the family of heaven.
> Let the ale be made from the fruits of faith,
> And the food be forgiving love.

I should welcome the poor to my feast,
For they are God's children.
I should welcome the sick to my feast,
For they are God's joy.
Let the poor sit with Jesus at the highest place,
And the sick dance with the angels.

God bless the poor,
God bless the sick,
And bless our human race.
God bless our food,
God bless our drink,
All homes, O God embrace.

("Brigid's Feast" in *Celtic Fire*
by Robert Van De Weyer, 39–40)

• • •

The symbolism of the messianic banquet appears again
and again in Scripture. We find it in the prophets, the parables of Jesus, the Passover meal, the institution of the Lord's
Supper, and the vision of the New Jerusalem. The God of
heaven and earth has prepared the feast and made all things
ready. Presiding as the host at the table is Jesus Christ. The
Holy Spirit gives the invitation to come. All are invited to
share the bounty that has been prepared. Only the best ingre-
dients are used—the finest flour, the fatted calf, the lamb
without blemish, and the choicest wine. All can take part
"without money and without price."

Here in the symbolism are clues as to what the designer of
the universe had in mind. The preferred role that God has
chosen is not that of a judge or warrior but of a generous host.
To celebrate a joyful, festive occasion such as the marriage of
an only son, God has invited the human race to come to a
wedding feast, the most festive of all occasions.

What lies behind the invitations? There is no hidden
agenda. God simply wants the guests to come to the palace

and enjoy his company for an evening of song and dance, entertainment and good food. Some choose to decline the invitation for many trivial reasons, but basically they do not come because they do not want to have fellowship with the heavenly Father or the other guests who have been invited.

The banquet table provides opportunity for both nourishment and fellowship, an occasion for conversation and the enjoyment of each other's company. In every culture, eating together symbolizes the cementing of relationships. Table hospitality means loyalty, solidarity, and communion.

The rich imagery of the messianic banquet extends from this earth to the heavenly kingdom. On earth, the banquet can be experienced only briefly and imperfectly. The Passover meal was eaten hurriedly and fearfully in the presence of the enemy. The Lord's Supper was eaten in the shadow of impending doom. But each meal was a foretaste of the coming banquet that will be celebrated in the leisure, security, and bounty of the heavenly kingdom.

The communion table stands between the two celebrations. Think of it as the "in-between table," the link between the last supper our Lord had with his disciples and the banquet that will be spread in heaven. At one end of this table, we sit and partake of bits of bread and sips of wine. We eat this meal in faith and in anticipation of the banquet to come. At the other end of the table, the church triumphant is seated. Loved ones, colleagues, and friends of long ago are gathered. Also gathered are people from other nations, tribes, and cultures, for the "in-between table" bridges the gap between those who come from all corners of the earth to sit at the table with Abraham. From time to time some of our number move from one end of the table to the other end. But it is the same table! The same host presides. The same gracious invitation is given: "Come, for all has been made ready."

Chapter 20

Songs, Old and New

*P*raise him with trumpet sound;
  praise him with lute and harp!
Praise him with tambourine and dance;
  praise him with strings and pipe!
Praise him with clanging cymbals;
  praise him with loud clashing cymbals!
Let everything that breathes praise the LORD!
          (Ps. 150:3–6, NRSV)

They sing the song of Moses, the servant of God,
And the song of the Lamb:
  "Great and amazing are your deeds,
    Lord God the Almighty!
  Just and true are your ways,
    King of the nations!
  Lord, who will not fear
    and glorify your name?
  For you alone are holy.
    All nations will come and worship before
    you. . . ."
          (Rev. 15:3–4, NRSV)

. . . I heard a voice from heaven like the sound of
many waters and like the sound of loud thunder; the
voice I heard was like the sound of harpists playing
on their harps, and they sing a new song before the
throne and before the four living creatures and before
the elders. . . . (Rev. 14:2–3, NRSV)

They sing a new song:
"You are worthy to take the scroll
    and to open its seals,
for you were slaughtered and by your blood you
    ransomed for God
    saints from every tribe and language and people and
        nation;
you have made them to be a kingdom and priests
    serving our God,
    And they will reign on earth."

Then I looked, and I heard the voice of many angels surrounding the throne and the living creatures and the elders; they numbered myriads of myriads and thousands of thousands, singing with full voice:

"Worthy is the Lamb that was slaughtered
to receive power and wealth and wisdom and might
and honor and glory and blessing!"

Then I heard every creature in heaven and on earth and under the earth and in the sea, and all that is in them, singing,

"To the one seated on the throne and to the Lamb
be blessing and honor and glory and might
forever and ever!"

(Rev. 5:9–13, NRSV)

• • •

Oh, the happiness of the heavenly alleluia,
    Sung in security,
    In fear of no adversity.
We shall have no enemies in heaven,
    We shall never lose a friend.
God's praises are sung both there and here;
    But here they are sung in anxiety,
    There, in security;
Here they are sung by those destined to die,

there by those destined to live forever;
Here they are sung in hope,
    there, in hope's fulfillment;
Here they are sung by wayfarers,
    there, by those living in their own country.
(Saint Augustine of Hippo in *Christian Prayer:*
                    The Liturgy of the Hours, 2039)

Before the Lord

Before the Lord I'm going to sing
I'm going to dance the Highland Fling.
I'll make some noise
I'll lose my poise
Before the Lord.

Before the Lord I'm going to shout.
I'm going to pull the throttle out.
I'll raise my voice.
How I'll rejoice
Before the Lord.

Before the Lord I'll shout my praise.
My voice, my hands, my feet, I'll raise.
I'll shout and scream.
I'll let off steam
Before the Lord.

How my God must love to laugh!
God makes the monkey, the giraffe.
The hippo and the chimpanzee.
God even fashioned you and me.
A God who makes the world a riot.
How can I celebrate with quiet?

Before the Lord I'll jump and spin.
I'll even get some whistling in.
I'm having fun.
I've just begun
Before the Lord!
        (Rex Knowles, *Monday Morning,* June 1993)

If all experienced God in the same way and returned Him an identical worship, the song of the Church triumphant would have no symphony, it would be like an orchestra in which all the instruments played the same note. (C. S. Lewis, *The Problem of Pain*, 138)

• • •

Everyone in heaven seems to be singing. Music fills the air. The four living creatures sing without ceasing of the holiness of God (Rev. 4:8). The twenty-four elders cast their crowns before the throne and sing of the mysteries of creation (Rev. 4:10–11). The angels surrounding the throne sing a song of thanksgiving to our God (Rev. 7:11–12). Reminiscent of a grand finale the hosts of heaven are joined by the great multitude of those on earth and under the earth and on the sea (Rev. 5:13).

They sing because language spoken in a monotone is inadequate to express feelings of joy, devotion, and thanksgiving. Prose falls short as a vehicle for communication. Rhyme comes closer. From the beginning of time people from every continent have turned to song to express their inmost desires and their hopes for the future. Music is the medium that best unites us with those of other cultures and other centuries.

There are no soloists in heaven. All present are part of the heavenly choir, each singing their own part. The popular image of music in heaven is that of angels playing on harps, but that is too limited and too tame. To the harp should be added the trumpet, the tambourine, the cymbal of ancient Israel, and today's musical instruments from every race and tribe. Add also the accompaniments of nature—the sound of many waters and the peal of thunder.

The music of heaven continues the songs of earth. The song of Moses, the Psalter, and the hymns of every age are still sung. But a new dimension has been added. The theme song is addressed to the lamb who was slaughtered and is yet alive. The lamb has broken the seals of history, which is now an open book, and has gathered saints from every tribe and language and people and nation to be a kingdom of priests forever.

Chapter 21

Passionate Love

> . . . *l*ove is strong as death,
>   passion fierce as the grave. . . .
> Many waters cannot quench love,
>   neither can floods drown it.
>   (S. of Sol. 8:6–7, NRSV)

For God so loved the world that he gave his only begotten Son, that whosoever believeth in him should not perish, but have everlasting life. For God sent not his Son into the world to condemn the world; but that the world through him might be saved. (John 3:16–17, KJV)

. . . God is love. (1 John 4:8, NRSV)

. . . In all these things we are more than conquerors through him who loved us. For I am convinced that neither death, nor life, nor angels, nor rulers, nor things present, nor things to come, nor powers, nor height, nor depth, nor anything else in all creation, will be able to separate us from the love of God in Christ Jesus our Lord. (Rom. 8:37–39, NRSV)

To him who loves us and freed us from our sins by his blood, and made us to be a kingdom, priests serving his God and Father, to him be glory and dominion forever and ever. Amen. (Rev. 1:5–6, NRSV)

• • •

Heaven is full of passion, of energy and dynamism. . . .
But to think of the love that made the worlds, the love that
became human, suffered alienation from itself and died to
save us rebels, the love that gleams through the fanatic joy
of Jesus' obedience to the will of His Father and that
shines in the eyes and lives of the saints—to think of this
love as any less passionate than our temporary and condi-
tioned passions "is a most disastrous fantasy." (Peter
Kreeft. *Everything You Ever Wanted to Know about
Heaven But Never Dreamed of Asking,* 132)

. . . a small boy who, on being told that the sexual life was
the highest bodily pleasure should immediately ask
whether you ate chocolates at the same time. On receiving
the answer "no," he might regard the absence of chocolates
as the chief characteristic of sexuality. In vain would you
tell him that the reason why lovers in their carnal raptures
don't bother with chocolates is that they have something
better to think of. The boy knows chocolates; he does not
know the positive thing that excludes it. We are in the same
position. We know the sexual life; we do not know, except
in glimpses, the other thing which, in Heaven, will leave no
room for it. (C. S. Lewis, *Miracles,* 190–91)

We can negotiate everything about the pavement, the map-
ping and the furniture of heaven. . . . But the love of God
after death is non-negotiable. (Martin Marty, *Time,* March
24, 1997)

> Jesus, the very thought of Thee
> With sweetness fills my breast;
> But sweeter far Thy face to see,
> And in thy promise rest.
>
> Jesus, our only joy be Thou,
> As Thou our prize wilt be;
> Jesus, be Thou our glory now,
> And through eternity.
> (Bernard of Clairvaux, 1091–1153)

Ah, Lord God, Thou holy lover of my soul,
When Thou comest into my heart,
All that is within me shall rejoice.
    (Thomas à Kempis, 1379–1471)

O Love that wilt not let me go, I rest my weary soul in
    Thee;
I give thee back the life I owe, That in Thine ocean
    depths its flow
May richer, fuller be.
    (George Matheson, 1882)

Love divine, all loves excelling, Joy of heaven, to earth
    come down,
Fix in us Thy humble dwelling, All Thy faithful mercies
    crown!
Jesus, Thou art all compassion, Pure unbounded love
    thou art;
Visit us with Thy salvation, Enter every trembling heart.

Finish, then Thy new creation; Pure and spotless let us
    be;
Let us see Thy great salvation, Perfectly restored in Thee;
Changed from glory into glory, Till in heaven we take
    our place,
Till we cast our crowns before Thee, Lost in wonder,
    love and praise.
    (Charles Wesley, 1747)

• • •

Love called forth the worlds into being, drove back the
forces of chaos, and watches intensely over its creation like a
father waiting for a wayward son or a mother hen brooding
over her chicks. Love suffers pain and alienation for a lost
creation. Love is an action verb and is never content with
idleness. Love is the dynamo of heaven, the energy that fuels
the divine powerhouse, and the creative force that even now
is forming a new heaven and a new earth.

How tragic that for all this dynamism and passion we have substituted twentieth-century imagery that is dull, insipid, and uninteresting. It is a Satanic triumph of the first order, writes Peter Kreeft, that we have taken away the fascination of the heavenly vision and substituted insipid pictures of fluffy clouds, sexless cherubs, harps and haloes, presided over by a pompous chairman of the bored (Kreeft, *Everything You Ever Wanted to Know about Heaven but Never Dreamed of Asking*, 19).

The New Testament imagery could hardly be more different, with its brilliant lights, choirs, jewels, trumpets, sea captains, marching armies, victory celebrations, banquets, marriage suppers, and passionate love. Whatever else one might think of the imagery of the book of Revelation, and much of it is awesome and even unintelligible, one could hardly think of it as being dull!

Bored in heaven? Never. "Because we are with God and God is Love. Even on earth, the only people who are never bored are lovers" (Kreeft, p. 50).

The divine passion of heaven is the source of all earthly loves. But our earthly loves are only a pale comparison of the fountainhead from which they came. For two thousand years, saints, mystics, and hymn writers have written of Jesus Christ as the divine lover. He is a lover who never lets go. No sacrifice is too great for the beloved. Nothing can separate us from this love, which is more intense, more durable, and more pleasurable than any of the loves we know on earth.

And if all this could be true, then in heaven there will never be a dull moment.

Chapter 22

Overflowing Joy

*T*he wilderness and the dry land shall be glad,
   the desert shall rejoice and blossom;
   like the crocus
it shall blossom abundantly,
   and rejoice with joy and singing. . . .
Everlasting joy shall be upon their heads;
   they shall obtain joy and gladness,
   and sorrow and sighing shall flee away.
                      (Isa. 35:1–2, 10, NRSV)

. . . He will swallow up death forever.
Then the Lord GOD will wipe away the tears from
   all faces. . . .
It will be said on that day,
   Lo, this is our God; we have waited for him. . . .
   Let us be glad and rejoice in his salvation.
                      (Isa. 25:7–9, NRSV)

Just so, I tell you, there will be more joy in heaven over one sinner who repents than over ninety-nine righteous persons who need no repentance. (Luke 15:7, NRSV)

Enter into the joy of your master. (Matt. 25:23, NRSV)

. . . No one will take your joy from you. . . . Ask and you will receive, so that your joy may be complete. (John 16:22–24, NRSV)

Rejoice and be glad, for your reward is great in heaven. (Matt. 5:12, NRSV)

> And I heard a loud voice from the throne saying,
> "See, the home of God is among mortals,
> He will dwell with them as their God;
> they will be his peoples,
> and God himself will be with them;
> he will wipe every tear from their eyes—.
> Death will be no more;
> mourning and crying and pain will be no more,
> for the first things have passed away."
>
> (Rev. 21:3–4, NRSV)

• • •

Question: What is the chief end of man?
Answer: Man's chief end is to glorify God, and to enjoy Him forever. (*The Shorter Catechism*, 1646)

Heaven is not dull; it is not static; it is not monochrome. It is an endless dynamic of joy in which one is ever more oneself as one was meant to be. (J. B. Russell, *Time*, March 24, 1997)

> O Holy City seen of John,
> Where Christ the Lamb doth reign,
> Within those foursquare walls shall come
> No night, no need nor pain,
> And when the tears are wiped from eyes
> That shall not weep again!
>   (W. Russel Bowie, *The Holy City*, 1882)

> All thy works with joy surround Thee,
> Earth and heaven reflect thy rays,
> Stars and angels sing around Thee,
> Center of Unbroken praise:
> Field and forest, vale and mountain,
> Flowery meadow, flashing sea,

Chanting bird and flowing fountain
Call us to rejoice in Thee.
(Henry van Dyke, *Hymn to Joy,* 1852–1933)

• • •

Scenes from the book of Revelation describe the elimina-
tion of conditions that stand in the way of joy. Pain, sorrow,
and mourning are no more. God himself will wipe away
every tear. The terror of night and the chaos of darkness has
disappeared. The sea that isolated John on the island of
Patmos and separated him from friends and loved ones is no
more. And the final enemy, Death, has been abolished.

Joy can thus be described as the absence of pain and suffering. To say what it is in positive terms is more difficult.
Perhaps it could be defined as the normal state of a community that is at peace with itself, the world, and God. Joy, to be
joy, must be shared, not kept to itself. It must overflow and
touch the lives of others. Joy must be given away in order to
be replenished. Just as the community of faith on earth shares
its pains and sorrows, so the community in heaven shares its
many joys. There is the joy of:

> Giving thanks to God (Rev. 11:16)
> Welcoming each newcomer into the fellowship
>   (Luke 15:5–7)
> The playfulness of children (Matt. 18:1–10)
> Reunion with ones friends (1 Thess. 4:13–18)
> The feeling of being fresh and clean (Rev. 7:13–14,
>   22:14)
> The fellowship of the banquet (Matt. 22:1–14, Rev.
>   19:7–9)
> Participation in the singing of the heavenly chorus
>   (Rev. 7:9–12)
> Good health of body, mind, and spirit (Rev. 21:4–7,
>   22:2)

The joy of fellowship that is shared (1 John 1:3–4)
Rewards and commendation for services rendered
    (Rev. 15:23)
Confidence of final victory (Rev. 19:11–21)
The mystical communion of saints on earth and in
    heaven (Heb. 12:1–2)

All this is summed up in the magnificent affirmation of the
Shorter Catechism. Our "chief end" is (1) first to "glorify
God" and (2) second to "enjoy God forever." Too often we
have neglected the second and made of the Christian experience something that is dull, dour, and depressing. The catechism makes no distinction between the enjoyment of God
on earth and in heaven, but it must begin here. What begins
here will then continue without interruption, forever. Only it
will grow better and better.

Chapter 23

Enduring Peace

*T*hey shall beat their swords into plowshares,
    and their spears into pruning hooks;
nation shall not lift up sword against nation,
    neither shall they learn war any more;
but they shall all sit under their own vines and
    under their own fig trees,
    and no one shall make them afraid;
for the mouth of the LORD of hosts has spoken.
                         (Micah 4:3–4, NRSV)

The wolf shall dwell with the lamb,
    and the leopard shall lie down with the kid,
and the calf and the lion and the fatling together,
    and a little child shall lead them.
The cow and the bear shall feed;
    their young shall lie down together;
    and the lion shall eat straw like the ox.
The suckling child shall play over the hole of the
    asp,
    and the weaned child shall put his hand on the
    adder's den.
They shall not hurt or destroy
    in all my holy mountain;
for the earth shall be full of the knowledge of the
    LORD
    as the waters cover the sea.
                         (Isa. 11:6–9, RSV)

And suddenly there was with the angel a multitude of the heavenly host praising God, and saying, Glory to God in the highest, and on earth peace, good will toward men. (Luke 2:13–14, KJV)

. . . Jesus came and stood among them and said, "Peace be with you." After he said this, he showed them his hands and his side. Then the disciples rejoiced when they saw the Lord. Jesus said to them again, "Peace be with you. . . ." (John 20:19–21, NRSV)

"Blessed are the peacemakers, for they will be called children of God." (Matt. 5:9, NRSV)

• • •

Is it a dream—this faith of ours that pleads
And pulses in our hearts, and bids us look,
Through mists of tears and time, to that great day
When wars shall cease upon the earth, and men
As brothers bound by love of man and God
Shall build a world as gloriously fair
As sunset skies, or mountains when they catch
The farewell kiss of evening on their heights?
(G. A. Studdard-Kennedy, "Is It a Dream?" in
Masterpieces of Religious Verse, 552)

• • •

Enduring peace has been the dream of prophets, patriots, and artists of every generation. Isaiah's charming vision of lions and oxen, little children and wild animals living and playing together became an obsession for the Quaker artist Edward Hicks, who during his lifetime painted over eighty versions of "The Peaceful Kingdom." In his later paintings the wild animals became even more ferocious, highlighting the author's wonder and awe that such a peaceful scene could ever come true.

Look at that other vision of peace from the prophet Micah. The scene is that of the nations beating their swords and spears into instruments of agriculture. A modern-day equivalent of Micah's vision appears in the recommendations of the Independent Commission on International Development chaired by Willie Brandt, the former mayor of Berlin. Brandt links the issue of disarmament with that of food production, as Micah did: "One half of one percent of one year's world military production would pay for all the farm equipment needed to increase food production and approach self-sufficient in food-deficit low income countries by 1990." (Willy Brandt: *North South: A Program for Survival,* 14)

Such a small step! Such a reasonable proposal with consequences that could lead to sufficient food supplies for starving millions! That was fifteen years ago, but today we are no nearer the fulfillment of the vision than was Micah.

In perhaps no other feature is the landscape of heaven so different from the landscape of earth. As this book is being written, armed conflicts have been fought in Kosovo, the Congo, Angola, Sudan, Somalia, Eritrea, Rwanda, East Timor, and Liberia. Peace negotiations have either failed or are on hold in North Ireland, Bosnia, Palestine, Chiapas, Iraq, and Kashmir. Discrimination and alienation of minorities and ethnic groups threaten the peace in Algeria, Turkey, Sri Lanka, the Philippines, Indonesia, and the United States of America. North Korea and the Taiwan Straits remain potential danger points for world conflict.

The prophetic vision of enduring peace points only toward the messianic era and the rule of the messianic king. The Prince of Peace would usher in an era of *shalom,* which would be not only the absence of armed conflict but also the health and well-being of all of God's children, for if some are left out, the peace would not hold. *Shalom* would solve the root problems of human greed, jealousy, exploitation, discrimination, and national pride. The vicious cycle of violence must be broken.

Will the dream ever come true? Little by little, the heavenly vision will unfold, giving hope and inspiration for those whom Jesus called the "peacemakers." Yes, the vision will come true, beginning with the making of peace with God. Martin Luther King Jr.'s dream of peace and equality across our land was based on his faith that in the Kingdom of God peace will prevail.

Some years ago I read in a Seoul newspaper the incredible story of a Japanese army sergeant who surrendered twenty-six years after the end of World War II. Two Guam fishermen found a strange, savage-looking man tending a fish trap in a mountain stream and took him to the nearest police station. Shoichi Yokoi, a fifty-eight-year-old sergeant in the imperial Japanese Army, told his story.

The battle for Guam was coming to a climax. He was cut off from his unit. Later he heard the loudspeakers proclaiming that the war was over. Peace had been declared. The killing could stop. All could go home. But Sgt. Yokoi had not believed what he had heard. He retreated further back into the jungle and dug a cave. He lived alone and fed himself on rats, snails, little fish, and nuts—for twenty-six years! How incredible! How unnecessary! All that time, he could have gone home!

Isn't this a parable of heaven and earth? Over nineteen hundred years ago the loudspeakers of heaven sounded the good news. The angelic host at Bethlehem proclaimed it: "Peace on earth, good will among all people." The war is over.

God is not angry with the human race. He is not counting our sins against us. He has declared an unconditional amnesty. In Christ he wants to reconcile the whole world to himself. You can leave the jungles of life where you hide. You can come out into the sunshine of God's love. All of God's children can come home.

Chapter 24

The City

*F*or he looked forward to the city that has foundations, whose architect and builder is God. . . . They confessed that they were strangers and foreigners on the earth, . . . They desire a better country, that is, a heavenly one. Therefore God is not ashamed to be called their God; indeed, he has prepared a city for them. (Heb. 11:10–16, NRSV)

Then I saw a new heaven and a new earth; for the first heaven and the first earth had passed away, and the sea was no more. And I saw the holy city, the new Jerusalem, coming down out of heaven from God, prepared as a bride adorned for her husband. . . . It has the glory of God and a radiance like a very rare jewel, like jasper, clear as crystal. It has a great, high wall with twelve gates, and at the gates twelve angels, and on the gates are inscribed the names of the twelve tribes of the Israelites. . . . And the wall of the city has twelve foundations, and on them are the twelve names of the twelve apostles of the Lamb.

The angel who talked to me had a measuring rod of gold to measure the city and its gates and walls. . . . and he measured the city with his rod, fifteen hundred miles; its length and width and height are equal. He also measured its wall, one hundred forty-four cubits by human measurement, which the angel was using. The wall is built of jasper, while the city is pure gold, clear as glass. The foundations of the wall of the city are adorned with every jewel. . . . And the

twelve gates are twelve pearls, each of the gates is a single
pearl, and the street of the city is pure gold, transparent as
glass. (Rev. 21:1–21, NRSV)

• • •

Jerusalem the Golden,
   With milk and honey blest,
Beneath thy contemplation,
   Sink heart and voice opprest.
I know not, O I know not,
   What joys await us there;
What radiance of glory,
   What bliss beyond compare.

They stand, those halls of Zion,
   All jubilant with song,
And bright with many an angel,
   And all the martyr throng.
The Prince is ever in them,
   The daylight is serene;
The pastures of the blessed
   Are decked in glorious sheen. . . .

O sweet and blessed country,
   The home of God's elect!
O sweet and blessed country
   That eager hearts expect!
Jesus, in mercy bring us
   To that dear land of rest;
Who art, with God the Father
   And Spirit, ever blest.
      (Bernard of Cluny, c. 1145)

• • •

Before we can make out the dim outlines of the city of
God, we must first confess that we are strangers and pilgrims
here. Here, we have no lasting city. We look for that city that
is to come. "Our citizenship," wrote the Apostle Paul, "is in

heaven" (Phil. 3:20, NRSV). Or, to use words describing life in modern-day America, here we are "resident aliens."

Yes, we love and honor the purple mountains and alabaster cities where we live. The prophet Jeremiah urged the exiles in Babylon to seek the welfare of the cities where they sojourned (Jer. 29:7). We too are to throw our lot in with the people where we live; yet we too confess that here we have no permanent abiding place.

The description of the city in John's vision may seem strange until we understand the symbolic nature of the writing. Symbols are not pictures. The picture of a bleeding lamb sitting on a throne is grotesque. But viewed as a symbol of the crucified and risen Christ who combines the gentleness of the lamb with the authority of the throne, the image moves us with awe and wonder.

The great high walls of the city stand for permanence, stability, and security. To the persecuted Christians of Asia Minor to whom John was writing, the image brought a sense of ultimate security. The city itself is "foursquare"—a perfect cube. Its tremendous size—fifteen hundred miles in length, width, and height—is, in the estimate of the prophet, large enough to accommodate all the peoples of the earth. There is room to spare. The act of measuring the city confirms that the design has been followed according to the most exacting specifications.

Inscribed on the gates of the city and its foundations are the names of the twelve tribes of Israel and the twelve apostles. There is continuity with the Israel of old, but the new city that is emerging is founded on the apostolic witness to Jesus Christ. Entrance into the city is provided by twelve gates, three on each side. The image is one of spaciousness and grandeur. The number twelve speaks of the catholicity of the church through all generations. The city is open; the gates are never closed during the daylight hours, and since there is no night, the gates are always open. The use of gold, precious stones, and pearls are symbols of unsurpassed beauty. Such building materials never tarnish, rust, or grow old.

The dominant image on which the vision rests is that of the proximity of God to mortal men and women. This daring idea reverses the prevailing concept of the Old Testament that God was distant and holy. Now God has pitched his tent and taken up residence right here among us!

> See, the home of God is among mortals.
>   He will dwell with them;
>   they will be his peoples,
>   and God himself will be with them.
>   (Rev. 21:3, NRSV)

An even more daring concept is the image of the "bride adorned for her husband." The husband is none other than the "Lamb": the symbolic representation of Jesus Christ. The "bride" is the "city": the collective people of God down through the centuries. The characteristics of the union are mutual love, fidelity, and joy.

When John saw his vision of the Holy City, the walls of Jerusalem had been breached and the city he loved had been sacked, destroyed, and burnt to the ground. Amid the ruins of the earthly city, John saw descending from heaven the walls of the city of God. Saint Augustine saw the collapse of the Roman Empire and the civilization of which he was a part. Out of the disintegration of all that he knew and loved came his great classic, *The City of God*. When the life around us with which we are familiar collapses into rubble, then we too may see the spires of the New Jerusalem descending from heaven.

Chapter 25

The Garden

*A*nd the Lẑẑẑ God planted a garden in Eden, in the east; and there he put the man whom he had formed. Out of the ground the Lord God made to grow every tree that is pleasant to the sight and good for food, the tree of life also in the midst of the garden, and the tree of the knowledge of good and evil.

A river flows out of Eden to water the garden, and from there it divides and becomes four branches. . . . The Lord God took the man and put him in the garden of Eden to till it and keep it. And the Lord God commanded the man, "You may freely eat of every tree of the garden; but of the tree of the knowledge of good and evil you shall not eat, for in the day that you eat of it you shall die." (Gen. 2:8–17, NRSV)

On the banks, on both sides of the river, there will grow all kinds of trees for food. Their leaves will not wither nor their fruit fail, but they will bear fresh fruit every month, because the water for them flows from the sanctuary. Their fruit will be for food, and their leaves for healing. (Ezek. 47:12, NRSV)

Then the angel showed me the river of the water of life, bright as crystal, flowing from the throne of God and of the Lamb through the middle of the street of the city. On either side of the river is the tree of life with its twelve kinds of fruit, producing its fruit each month; and the leaves of the tree are for the healing of the nations. Nothing accursed will be found there any more. (Rev. 22:1–3, NRSV)

• • •

And then all that has divided us will merge
And then compassion will be wedded to power
And then softness will come to a world that is harsh and
    unkind
And then both men and women will be gentle
And then both women and men will be strong
And then no person will be subject to another's will
And then the greed of some will give way to the needs of
    others
And then all will share equally in the Earth's abundance
And then all will care for the sick and the weak and the old
And then all will nourish the young
And then all will cherish life's creatures
And then all will live in harmony with each other and the
    Earth
And then everywhere will be called Eden once again.
             (Judy Chicago, "Merger" in *The Dinner Party:*
                            A Symbol of Our Heritage)

• • •

The human race has never forgotten that garden east of Eden. In the corporate memory of humanity there still lingers:

The pristine loveliness of each new morning,
The lush foliage,
The beauty of the trees,
The taste of the fruit,
The friendly animals coming by to get their names,
The pleasant task of tilling the fertile fields,
The mysterious trees in the center of the forest,
The love of a man for a woman and a woman for a man,
And the sound of the Lord God walking in the garden at
    the time of the evening breeze.

Then all was lost. Our first parents were expelled from the garden. The Lord God must have followed them out, for he fashioned skins for them and clothed them. Did the Lord God ever go back into the Garden? I wonder. What was there to go back to? Is there any way to start over again?

Yes, there is. For the Lord God never forgot that garden east of Eden. There it is in the vision of the Apocalypse—right in the center of the city of the New Jerusalem—the trees, the fruit, and life-giving water clear as crystal, flowing from the throne of God.

Every city needs a garden. And the New Jerusalem is no exception. The teeming multitudes of a metropolis need a place to find solitude, silence, and calm. Some of earth's rural peoples might not feel quite at home in a city paved over with gold and whose gates are of jewels. A garden presents a different kind of beauty.

In the vision John bypasses all the turbulent years of human conflict and reaches back to the dawn of history and to how it all began. The paradise that was lost has now been regained—regained and much more added! Nature's wondrous productivity is beyond our imagination. The tree of life has become twelve trees, each bearing its own fruit with its own distinctive taste. And each bears its fruit not in an annual harvest but twelve times every year. The tree of the "knowledge of good and evil" that had been the source of temptation has now disappeared. Any of the fruit can be eaten, without prohibition. The "curse" that had poisoned the garden has now been removed. All thorns and weeds, typhoons and monsoons, floods and droughts have disappeared. Harmony between humans and the environment has been restored.

In Genesis, the Lord God visited Eden and "walked in the garden at the time of the evening breeze." In Revelation, God does not just visit the garden; he has come there to dwell.

The time foretold by the prophet Ezekiel has now become a reality: "the leaves are for healing." John adds that the healing is "for the nations." The garden has now become coextensive with the world. The gates have been thrown wide open. The nations from the ends of the earth will come to the garden and be healed! The healing will be from disease and pestilence, river blindness, Alzheimer's, cancer, the AIDS epidemic, multiple sclerosis, Parkinson's disease, and much, much more. Healing takes place without restriction, so we hasten to add the curse of our warring madness, the vicious cycle of violence, the arrogance of national pride, and the fragmentation caused by ancient rivalries that tear us apart.

The vision ends with an invitation for all to "come" to the garden, "come" to eat of the fruit of the trees, "come" to be healed, "come" to enjoy the harmony with nature, "come" to renew fellowship with the One who dwells there.

Chapter 26

No Temple There

*T*hen the cloud covered the tent of meeting, and the glory of the LORD filled the tabernacle. Moses was not able to enter the tent of meeting because the cloud settled upon it, and the glory of the LORD filled the tabernacle. (Ex. 40:34–35, NRSV)

I hate, I despise your festivals,
    and I take no delight in your solemn assemblies.
Even though you offer me your burnt offerings and
        grain offerings,
    I will not accept them. . . .
Take away from me the noise of your songs;
    I will not listen to the melody of your harps.
But let justice roll down like waters,
    and righteousness like an ever flowing stream.
                                        (Amos 5:21–24, NRSV)

And he entered the temple and began to drive out those who were selling and those who were buying in the temple, and he overturned the tables of the money changers . . . saying, "Is it not written,

'My house shall be called a house of prayer for all
    the nations'?
But you have made it a den of robbers."
                                        (Mark 11:15–17, NRSV)

. . . the hour is coming when you will worship the Father neither on this mountain nor in Jerusalem. . . But the hour is coming, and is now here, when the

true worshipers will worship the Father in Spirit and truth,
. . . (John 4:21–23, NRSV)

Then Jesus cried again with a loud voice and breathed his
last. At that moment the curtain of the temple was torn in
two, from top to bottom. (Matt. 27:50–51, NRSV)

And all the angels stood around the throne and around the
elders and the four living creatures, and they fell on their
faces before the throne and worshiped God, singing,
> "Amen! Blessing and glory and wisdom
> and thanksgiving and honor
> and power and might
> be to our God forever and ever! Amen."
(Rev. 7:11–12, NRSV)

I saw no temple in the city, for its temple is the Lord
God the Almighty and the Lamb. And the city has no
need of sun or moon to shine on it, for the glory of God
is its light, and its lamp is the Lamb. (Rev. 21:22–23,
NRSV)

• • •

The most surprising feature of the "New Jerusalem" is that
John saw no temple there. Amazing! From beginning to end,
the book of Revelation is full of people worshipping. Why is
there no temple? The elders, the living creatures, the multitudes from every tribe and language and people are busy day
and night in worship. Earlier in the vision the temple is present. John is given a measuring rod and commanded to measure the temple (Rev. 11:1). But when we come to the
climactic description of the holy city coming down out of
heaven, the temple has disappeared.

What has happened?

Worship is about our search for intimacy with God. For
this is the reason we were created. Intimacy with God is our
destiny, but there is one huge problem. How can sinful, mor-

tal, human beings draw near to the awesome God who dwells in eternity and whose name is Holy?

In every religion, worship of the deity requires a careful proscribed pattern. Certain things are taboo. Certain procedures must be followed. Sacrifices must be brought. A special kind of place called a temple is designated for the meeting place of God and human beings. Only certain people, the priests, can fulfill the required functions.

For the Hebrew people, sacred space was first provided by their tabernacle in the wilderness. Its construction carefully followed the model shown to Moses on the mount. Meticulous instructions were given for the bread, the candlesticks, the altar, the animals to be sacrificed, feast days, and fast days. Later, came the temple in Jerusalem—bigger but the same dimensions were followed. Proximity to the holy of holies was limited to the high priest. Other priests could come only as far as the holy place. Women could only come so far. Gentiles were excluded. The sharp distinction between the sacred and the common had to be strictly enforced. Ordinary people needed to be shielded from the blazing light of God's holiness.

Yet from the beginning the temple system had problems. The system opened the door for empty formalism, for the corruption of the priesthood, and for worship that was not supported by acts of justice and mercy. Amos denounced the system in the strongest possible language: "I hate and despise your festivals." Jesus Christ followed the prophetic tradition by his symbolic acts of "cleansing the temple." Then came his death on the cross and the profoundly moving statement that the thick curtain that had always hung between the temple's holy place and the holy of holies had been ripped apart from top to bottom. Distinctions between "holy" and "holy of holies" were no more. The death of Jesus had provided free access to all! Each person, Jew or Gentile, could be one's own high priest.

That John in his vision saw no temple in the city should then come as no surprise. The city needs no temple because the presence of God and of the Lamb is continually there. After all, a temple is a place that is set apart so that people may specially meet God there; but in the city of God there was no need for such a place, for the presence of God and of Jesus Christ was never lacking and never lost (William Barclay, *The Revelation of John,* vol. 2, 275).

The whole city was alive with the worship of God, so a temple would only have been in the way! God, in person, now dwells among God's people. Worship can now take place without the props of temple, sacrifice, high priests, incense, or altars. True believers anywhere in heaven or on earth can now worship in "spirit and in truth."

Chapter 27

The Glory and Honor of the Nations

*Y*our gates shall always be open;
   day and night they shall not be shut,
so that nations shall bring you their wealth,
   with their kings led in procession.
                    (Isa. 60:11, NRSV)

The city has no need of sun or moon to shine on it,
for the glory of God is its light, and its lamp is the
Lamb. The nations will walk by its light, and the
kings of the earth will bring their glory into it. Its
gates will never be shut by day—and there will be no
night there. People will bring into it the glory and
honor of the nations. But nothing unclean will enter
it. . . . (Rev. 21:23–27, NRSV)

After this I looked, and there was a great multitude
that no one could count, from every nation, from all
tribes and peoples and languages, standing before the
throne and before the Lamb, robed in white. . . .
(Rev. 7:9, NRSV)

• • •

From earth's wide bounds,
From ocean's farthest coast,
Through gates of pearl
Stream in the countless hosts,
Singing to Father, Son and Holy Ghost,
Alleluia! Alleluia!
         (William Walsham How, 1864)

Booth led boldly with his big bass drum—
(Are you washed in the blood of the lamb?)
The Saints smiled gravely and they said: "He's come."
(Are you washed in the blood of the lamb?)
Walking lepers followed, rank on rank,
Lurching bravos from the ditches dank,
Drabs from the alleyways and drug fiends pale—
Minds still passion-ridden, soul-powers frail:–
Vermin-eaten saints with moldy breath,
Unwashed legions with the ways of Death—
(Are you washed in the blood of the lamb?). . .

Round and round the mighty court house square
Then, in an instant all that blear review
Marched on spotless, clad in raiment new.
The lame were straightened, withered limbs uncurled
And blind eyes opened on a new, sweet world. . . .
Sages and sibyls now, and athletes clean,
Rulers of empires and of forest green!
Oh shout Salvation! It was good to see
Kings and Princes by the lamb set free.
Are you washed in the blood of the lamb?
        (Vachel Lindsay, "General William Booth Enters
        Heaven," in *Masterpieces of Religious Verse,* 505)

Aristotle has told us that a city is a unity of unlikes, and St.
Paul that a body is a unity of different members. Heaven
is a city, and a Body, because the blessed remain eternally
different: a society, because each has something to tell all
the others—fresh and ever fresh news of the "My God"
whom each finds in Him whom all praise as "Our God."
(C. S. Lewis, *The Problem of Pain,* 138)

John, like the ancient prophets, repeatedly speaks of the
Gentiles and their kings bringing their gifts and their
honour to God. . . . The Greeks brought their power of
their intellect. . . . The Romans were the greatest jurists
and the great experts in government. . . . To the Church
they brought their ability to organize and to administer

and to formulate law. . . . There is no gift which Christ can not use, and to His Church men must bring all their gifts, and the Church must learn more than ever to welcome and use them. (William Barclay, *The Revelation of John,* vol. 2, 280)

• • •

All the tribes, nations, clans, and peoples of the world will be there. Even tribes as yet unborn will be included. The high and mighty, the weak and lowly . . . all will be there. Saints and sinners, youths and oldsters, athletes and children—all will be marching in the great procession. General William Booth of the Salvation Army leads the parade as his legions enter the pearly gates. What a stupendous sight it will be! The African spiritual captures the excitement of the moment: "Lord, I want to be in that number, when the saints go marching in!"

As astonishing as the diversity of the huge procession is the nature of the gifts they bring. As the wise men of old each brought different presents, so each has something unique to offer. They will bring into the city the "glory and the honor of the nations." Each will have some distinctive gift that represents the culture out of which they have come.

But surely the city—its gates and walls emblazoned with sapphires, topaz, amethyst, pearls, and emeralds—needs nothing more. And if it did, the architect could supply it out of the treasure house. What does it mean—this "glory and honor of the nations" that is brought by the kings and captains, the emperors, and chiefs from the ends of the earth?

Just this: The new Jerusalem will be a multicultural city. No one culture can claim preeminence. The ethos of the city will reflect the national honor and glory of all the traditions of the people who come marching into its gates. Jews will still be Jews. Americans will still be Americans. Koreans will be Koreans. Yes, they will now all be citizens of the new city that is not divided into "Latin," "Armenian," "Christian," "Jewish," or "Palestinian" quarters. But no group will lose anything that is noble and good from its own tradition.

To say it another way, our understanding of the beauty and fullness of the heavenly vision will remain incomplete until each ethnic group brings into the gates of the city its own gifts of glory and honor! Each reader will want to supply their own list. Here is mine:

> Koreans will bring their enthusiasm for witness.
> Africans—their sense of awe and mystery in the presence of Spirit.
> Chinese—their devotion to family values.
> Japanese—their sense of politeness and hospitality.
> Latin Americans—their joy in worship and celebrations.
> And, of course, the Jews, to whom Gentiles owe everything.

Only when all the tribes and peoples of the earth have brought into the city their "glory and honor" will the vision be complete.

Chapter 28

The Throne

> . . . *t*he LORD sits enthroned forever,
>   he has established his throne for judgment.
> He judges the world with righteousness;
>   he judges the peoples with equity.
>   (Ps. 9:7–8, NRSV)

"When the Son of Man comes in his glory, and all the angels with him, then he will sit on the throne of his glory. All the nations will be gathered before him, and he will separate people one from another as a shepherd separates the sheep from the goats, and he will put the sheep at his right hand and the goats at the left." (Matt. 25:31–32, NRSV)

Then I saw a great white throne and the one who sat on it; the earth and the heaven fled from his presence, and no place was found for them. And I saw the dead, great and small, standing before the throne, and books were opened. . . . And the dead were judged according to their works, as recorded in the books. (Rev. 20:11–13, NRSV)

For all of us must appear before the judgment seat of Christ. . . . (2 Cor. 5:10, NRSV)

If God is for us, who is against us? He who did not withhold his own Son, but gave him up for all of us, will he not with him also give us everything else? Who will bring any charge against God's elect? It is

God who justifies. Who is to condemn? It is Christ Jesus,
who died, yes, who was raised, who is at the right hand of
God, who indeed intercedes for us. Who will separate us
from the love of Christ? (Rom. 8:31–35, NRSV)

There is therefore now no condemnation for those who are
in Christ Jesus. For the law of the Spirit of life in Christ
Jesus has set you free from the law of sin and of death.
(Rom. 8:1–2, NRSV)

• • •

We believe in one God. . . . and in the Lord Jesus Christ .
. . who ascended into heaven, and sitteth on the right hand
of the Father. And he shall come again with glory to judge
both the quick and the dead. . . . (The Nicene Creed)

To believe in eternal life means—in reasonable trust, in
enlightened faith, in tried and tested hope—to rely on the
fact that I shall one day be fully understood, freed from
guilt and definitively accepted, and can be myself without fear. . . . (Hans Kung, *Eternal Life? Life after Death
as a Medical, Philosophical, and Theological Problem,*
231)

• • •

The most perplexing imagery of the Apocalypse is that of
the Lamb "standing as if it had been slaughtered" at the center of the throne. Again and again the image of the throne and
the image of the Lamb are brought together. The "throne"
speaks of the power, authority, and majesty of God. The
Lamb speaks of weakness, vulnerability, meekness, and sacrifice. To put the two together seems contradictory.

The imagery becomes all the more striking when we
remember that the "throne" is the seat of God's final act of
judgment. The One seated on the throne and the Lamb speak
as one voice to proclaim the judgment. For some the judg-

ment comes as vindication and deliverance. For others the judgment comes as the voice of doom. Some of "the rich and powerful" of the earth cry out to the rocks to "fall on us and hide us from . . . the wrath of the Lamb" (Rev. 6:15–16, NRSV). Others who have suffered from the scorching heat of oppression see the same Lamb at the center of the throne as a shepherd who guides them to the springs of the water of life (Rev. 7:17).

Judgment is something we would rather not think about. "Is it really necessary?" we instinctively ask. Yes, judgment is absolutely necessary. It appears too often in the Scriptures of the Old and New Testament to be dismissed. Jesus speaks of the coming judgment in a number of different ways: as the settlement of accounts (Matt. 25:14–30), the division of sheep and goats (Matt. 25:31–32), or the gathering in of the harvest (Matt. 13:24–30).

We accept the necessity of judgments here on earth. But here, even at best, judgments are flawed, partial, and incomplete. Too often judgments are made in ignorance before all the facts are known. A final judgment will and must take place. The tangled threads of history must be sorted out. Some kind of summing up or closure must take place. In fact, judgment is something we should welcome in order to close the books on the past and make a new beginning.

Judgment is necessary. And yet we must quickly add that it will be like nothing we have known or experienced. With all the difficulty our finite minds have understanding the final judgment, from Scripture some things are clear:

- The judgment is certain. It will include all humankind, with no exceptions. All individuals, nations, races, and peoples will be judged.
- We will not be doing the judging. Again and again we are warned not to pronounce judgment on others. "Judge not, that you be not judged" (Matt. 7:1, RSV).

- The judgment has been delayed because of the ever-lasting mercy of God (Matt. 13:24–30, NRSV). God wills the salvation of all and takes no delight in the loss of any of his children.
- The judgment will be fair and equitable. No grain of wheat will be judged a weed and no weed will be judged a grain of wheat (Matt. 13:24–30, NRSV).
- Judgment will be based on deeds, not profession. "Not everyone who says to me 'Lord, Lord' . . . but only the one who does the will of my Father in heaven" (Matt. 7:22, NRSV).
- Judgment will be in accordance with the opportunities that have been received. Those "under the law" will be judged by the law. Those "without the law" will be judged according to the law written on their hearts (Rom. 2:1–29, NRSV). More is expected of those to whom more has been given (Matt. 25:14–30, NRSV).
- For many of the downtrodden and oppressed who never had their chance at a "fair deal" in this life, the last judgment will be a time of liberation.
- The outcome of the judgment is linked to how we forgive each other. In order to experience the joy of God's free grace in forgiving the enormous debts we owe to God, we must forgive the trifling debts that are owed to us by our fellow human beings (Matt. 18:21–35, NRSV).
- For those "in Christ," the judgment holds no terror and no fear. Jesus said, "I will never refuse anyone who comes to me" (John 6:37, PHILLIPS).

Chapter 29

Face to Face

> *S*o God created humankind in his image,
> in the image of God he created them;
> male and female he created them.
>
> (Gen. 1:27, NRSV)

[T]he LORD used to speak to Moses face to face, as one speaks to a friend. (Ex. 33:11, NRSV)

Moses said, "Show me your glory, I pray." And he [God] said, "I will make all my goodness pass before you . . . but . . . you cannot see my face; for no one shall see me and live." And the LORD continued, "See, there is a place by me where you shall stand on the rock; and while my glory passes by I will put you in a cleft in the rock, and I will cover you with my hand until I have passed by; then I will take away my hand, and you shall see my back; but my face shall not be seen." (Ex. 33:18–23, NRSV)

Never since has there arisen a prophet in Israel like Moses, whom the LORD knew face to face. (Deut. 34:10, NRSV)

"Blessed are the pure in heart, for they will see God." (Matt. 5:8, NRSV)

What we do know is this: when he is revealed, we will be like him, for we will see him as he is. (1 John 3:2, NRSV)

For we know in part and we prophesy in part.

But when that which is perfect is come, then that which is in part shall be done away.

When I was a child, I spake as a child, I understood as a child, I thought as a child: but when I became a man, I put away childish things.

For now we see through a glass, darkly; but then face to face: now I know in part; but then shall I know even as also I am known.

And now abideth faith, hope, charity, these three; but the greatest of these is charity. (1 Cor. 13:9–13, KJV)

But the throne of God and of the Lamb will be in it, and his servants will worship him; they will see his face, and his name will be on their foreheads. (Rev. 22:3–4, NRSV)

• • •

The Master said: if a man in the morning knows the . . . Way [*Tao*], he may die in the evening without regret. (Confucius, 478 B.C., *The Analects,* chapter 4, verse 8)

> O Christ, whom now beneath a veil we see,
> May what we thirst for soon our portion be,
> To gaze on Thee unveiled,
> And see Thy face,
> the vision of Thy glory and Thy grace.
> (Thomas Aquinas, 1225–74)

Sunset and evening star,
And one clear call for me!
And may there be no moaning of the bar,
When I put out to see, . . .

Twilight and evening bell,
And after that the dark!
And may there be no sadness of farewell
When I embark;

For tho' from out our bourne of Time and Place
The flood may bear me far,

I hope to see my Pilot face to face
When I have crossed the bar.
                    (Alfred Tennyson, 1809–1892)

It is safe to tell the pure in heart that they shall see God,
for only the pure in heart want to. (C. S. Lewis, *The
Problem of Pain,* 133)

> Give us
> A pure heart
> That we may see Thee
> A humble heart
> That we may hear Thee,
> A heart of love
> That we may serve Thee,
> A heart of faith
> That we may live Thee,
> Thou. . .
>   (Dag Hammarskjöld, *Markings,* 214)

• • •

For the knights of the round table, it was the quest of the
Holy Grail. For the Chinese philosophers it was the mysterious Tao. For the Norsemen, it was Valhalla, the hall of the
heroes. For Muslims it is the pilgrimage to Mecca and the
black rock. People from different cultures, religions, and traditions have always sensed that there was "a something" at
the end of the quest that beckoned to them.

Surely, for the writers of the Scriptures it was a face, not a
thing or a place or a philosophical idea but the face of God.
For pilgrims along the way, the face both attracted and
repelled. The thought of coming face to face—one on one—
with God fills us with dread and we seek, as Moses did, to
hide our faces behind a veil or in the cleft of the rock. But the
face also has had a fascination that is irresistible.

This attraction can be traced back to the way we were
created. Each of us has been created in the image of God.

That image has been defaced, but it will be restored once again. I will be "like him" for I will "see him as he is," face to face.

Now we are as those "looking at puzzling reflections in a mirror. The time will come when we shall see reality whole and face to face" (1 Cor. 13:12, PHILLIPS). Today we confuse the "real" with that which is imaginary. But one day the veil will be lifted and we will see it all without distortion. "At present all I know is a little fraction of the truth, but the time will come when I shall know it as fully as God has known me" (1 Cor. 13:12, PHILLIPS). Today we see everything through the eyes of a child, but the time is coming when it will be time to put away the toys and learn what else God wants to teach us.

At the center of the universe is a human face that knows me! The smiling, friendly face that understands my human condition and calls me by name is the face of Jesus Christ.

But some things don't change. Our three old friends— faith, hope, and love—that have been the markers along the way of our pilgrimage will continue to guide us throughout eternity.

Chapter 30

More

*F*or since the beginning of the world men have not heard, nor perceived by the ear, neither hath the eye seen, O God, beside thee, what he hath prepared for him that waiteth for him. (Isa. 64:4, KJV)

. . . far more than all we can ask or imagine. . . . (Eph. 3:20, NRSV)

I consider that the sufferings of this present time are not worth comparing with the glory about to be revealed to us. For the creation waits with eager longing for the revealing of the children of God. (Rom. 8:18, NRSV)

Beloved, we are God's children now; what we will be has not yet been revealed. (1 John 3:2, NRSV)

But as it is written,

"What no eye has seen, nor ear heard,
   nor the human heart conceived,
      what God has prepared for those who love him. . ."
                                        (1 Cor. 2:9, NRSV)

• • •

Take the sum total of all past and present human experience, the entire universe, all of space and time and history and matter and mind—everything anyone has ever experienced. Add to it all future possibilities that we or any other creatures can or may experience on earth or in space or on other planets for billions of years to come until all the stars grow cold. Add an infinite number of evolutionary cycles, big bangs, and new universes if you like. Let us call this quantity of reality X. It is a partially unknown quantity but also partially known. Now let us ask of X: *Is that all there is?* Heaven is the negative answer to that question. There is more. (Kreeft, *Everything You Ever Wanted to Know about Heaven but Never Dreamed of Asking,* 22)

A woman who had been diagnosed with cancer was given three months to live. Her doctor told her to start making preparations to die, so she contacted her pastor and had him come to her house to discuss certain aspects of her final wishes. She told him which songs she wanted sung at the service, what scriptures she would like read, and what she wanted to be wearing. Everything was in order and the pastor was preparing to leave when the woman suddenly remembered something very important to her. "There is one more thing," she said excitedly. "What's that?" came the pastor's reply. "This is very important," the woman continued. "I want to be buried with a fork in my right hand." The pastor stood looking at the woman not knowing what to say. "That shocks you, doesn't it?" the woman asked. "Well, to be honest, I'm puzzled by the request," said the pastor. The woman explained, "In all my years of attending church socials and functions when food was involved, my favorite part was when whoever was clearing away the dishes would lean over and say, "You can keep your fork." It was my favorite part because I knew that something better was coming. When they told me to keep my fork, I knew that something great was about to be given to me. It wasn't Jell-O or pudding. It was cake or pie. So I just want people to see me there in that casket with a fork in my hand and I want them to wonder, "What's with the fork?" Then I want you to tell them: "Something better is coming." (Thanks to Charlotte Brown Hill, 1999)

Here in this present human life we are permitted to know something of beauty, truth, and goodness, to read something of the ultimate plan and meaning of the universe, and to see something of the splendor of the majesty of God. Yet the very best that we can see and know on earth is but a poor fraction of what must be waiting yonder to be revealed.

We can find a parable of this in modern science. There are whole ranges of colour, the scientist tells us, which our physical eyes cannot perceive. . . . In short, what we do see is a tiny segment of the whole. If this is true of our physical eyes, is it not likely to be true of the inner eye of our soul? . . . And beyond the best insights we can ever hope to have in this dark, shadowed existence of time and sin and limitation, what reaches of glory must be waiting for us yonder in the morning! We are going to find the answers to all questions unanswered here. We are to see the dearest faces we have loved and lost. We are to gaze upon that one Face which has haunted the dreams of humanity since the day when God walked with men in Galilee. . . . (James S. Stewart, *The Strong Name*, 248–49)

I have no idea what it will be like, and I think I am glad that I have not, as I am sure it would be wrong. . . [But] there is nothing in the world of which I am more certain. I do not mean that I want it for myself as mere continuance, but I want it for my understanding of life . . . also, I hope I may somewhere get further in likeness to God. (Archbishop William Temple in the year of his death quoted by Walter Russell Bowie, *Christ Be with Me*, 130–31.)

• • •

In our thinking on eternal life, I believe two extremes are to be avoided. One is the minimalist view: Heaven is a subject that should be dodged whenever possible, except at funerals when it can't be avoided. The other extreme is to engage in ceaseless debates on times and seasons, the rapture, the millennium, the pavement of the streets, and the furniture of the mansions. The latter danger was accelerated with the flurry of speculations regarding the "Y2K crisis." But this problem is not just one of modern times, as it was addressed over four hundred years ago by John Calvin, who warned against people who "investigated useless questions" and left "not a corner of heaven unexplored" (*Institutes,* III. 25. 11).

Our knowledge of the future life is partial, incomplete, and probably distorted.

A view of the future can only be expressed in symbols, images, parables, and visions. What we do know has been given for the specific purpose of equipping us for discipleship here and now. More than that we do not need to know.

An element of awe and mystery, surprise and anticipation add excitement to the Christian life. The thrill of discovery lies ahead. We are told that the whole creation is waiting with eager longing for what is going to happen to the human race. What we are now is clear. We are God's children. That will not change. But what else God has in store for each of us has not yet been revealed.

The key to our thinking of the future is the word "more." The Christian faith is the only religion that affirms that life after death will be "more" than it was before death. In what ways it will be "more" we cannot tell. But it will be "more" and not "less." It will be "more" than distant galaxies or Jell-O and pudding. It will be "more" than the sum total of all we have seen or heard or imagined in our wildest dreams. Take any noun you wish to describe our present reality and for the future you can add the word "more"—more joy, more beauty, more love, more kindness, more holiness, etc.

Nothing has been able to separate us from the love of God in this life. That love has overflowed in abundance to more than meet our human needs. What reasons do we have for placing limitations and restrictions on that love in the life which is to come?

Chapter 31

On Earth as in Heaven

*I*n the beginning, God created the heavens and the
earth. . . . God saw everything that he had made, and
behold, it was very good. (Gen. 1:1, 31, RSV)

> For I am about to create new heavens
> and a new earth. . . .
>   (Isa. 65:17, NRSV)

Pray then in this way:
   "Our Father, in heaven, hallowed be your name.
   Your kingdom come. Your will be done
   On earth as it is in heaven. . . ."
                 (The Lord's Prayer, Matt. 6:9–10, NRSV)

"The kingdom of the world has become the kingdom
   of our Lord
   and of his Messiah,
   and he will reign forever and ever."
                             (Rev. 11:15, NRSV)

Then I saw a new heaven and a new earth; for the
first heaven and the first earth had passed away. . . .
(Rev. 21:1, NRSV)

• • •

If I believe in an eternal life, then, in all modesty and
all realism . . . I can work for a better future, a better
society, even a better church, in peace, freedom, and

justice—knowing that all this can only be sought and never fully realized by man.

If I believe in an eternal life, I know that this world is not the ultimate reality, conditions do not remain as they are forever. All that exists—including both political and religious institutions—has a provisional character, the divisions into classes and races, poor and rich, rulers and ruled, remain temporary; the world is changing and changeable.

If I believe in an eternal life, then it is always possible to endow my life and that of others with meaning. In belief in God, however, as he showed himself in Jesus of Nazareth, I must start out from the fact that there can be a true consummation and a true happiness of humanity only when not merely the last generation but the full number of human beings—including those who have suffered, wept, and shed their blood in the past—will share in it. Not a human kingdom, but only God's kingdom is the kingdom of consummation: the kingdom of definitive salvation, of fulfilled justice, of perfect freedom, of unequivocal truth, of universal peace, of infinite love, of overflowing joy—in a word, of eternal life. (Hans Kung, *Eternal Life? Life after Death as a Medical, Philosophical, and Theological Problem*, 231–32)

What difference does Heaven make to earth, to now, to our lives? Only the difference between hope and despair in the end, between two totally different visions of life, between "chance or the dance." At death we find out which vision is true; does it all go down the drain in the end, or are all the loose threads finally tied together into a gloriously perfect tapestry? Do the tangled paths through the forest of life lead to the golden castle or over the cliff and into the abyss? Is death a door or a hole? (Kreeft, *Everything You Ever Wanted to Know about Heaven but Never Dreamed of Asking*, 17)

• • •

Every day millions of Christians the world over pray the prayer that our Lord taught us: "Thy kingdom come, thy will be done on earth as it is in heaven." Each time we pray the prayer we are asking God to make the kingdoms of this world a little more like the kingdom of heaven. This call is not for a crusade for political, social, or economic reforms, but rather a call for intercessory prayer. Yet it would be sheer hypocrisy to pray the prayer if one does not make a commitment to the object for which we are praying. Heaven is the vision of the coming kingdom here on earth. Heaven is the way the earth will become one day.

"On earth as it is in heaven." In spite of the vast differences of time and space and obedience to God's will, one can become like the other! This transformation is truly astounding, and yet it must be in the realm of possibility. Otherwise the Lord would not have asked us to pray for it. John's vision on Patmos includes them both: "I saw a new heaven and a new earth." Throughout the Scriptures, "heaven" and "earth" are never set one over against the other but are linked. To choose heaven does not mean to abandon the earth. The phrasing is not "either . . . or" but "both . . . and."

The idea that heaven is an escape route from the perils, injustices, and vicissitudes of earth is totally foreign to the Bible. The Marxist critique that the Christian idea of heaven is "pie in the sky by and by"—and that this draws our attention away from the injustices and problems of this earth—is a travesty. The cultic vision of a spacecraft hovering behind a meteor waiting to take a band of disillusioned individuals to a safe haven beyond the farthest star is idolatry and has nothing to do with the biblical doctrine of life, death, and resurrection.

Throughout history, prophets, crusaders, and revolutionaries have been among those for whom heaven has been most real. The prayer, "On earth as in heaven," serves as an effective motivator for righting the wrongs of earth. The vision of heaven gives no blueprint for reforms, yet the vision is a powerful projection of what God had in mind when the heavens and the earth were first created and the Creator pronounced them both "good."

This vision of heaven has immense implications for life here and now. The vision serves as a lever—a fulcrum—through which the earth can be moved inch by inch to become a little more like heaven. As long as we are here on earth and pray the prayer Jesus taught us, the vision of heaven that we have glimpsed in these brief meditations motivates us to make the vision a reality on earth.

If worship in heaven is the joyful, exciting, exuberant celebration of our intimate relationship with God in song, and prayer, and praise . . .

Then here on earth, worship must and can be something more than the dull, boring, repetitive ritual we sometimes make of it.

If the "fellowship of the saints" in heaven is the state in which all are united in love to one another and to God. . .

Then here on earth, the body of believers can and must become a visible unity of the one God, the one faith, and the one baptism.

If the heavenly community includes those from every nation, tribe, and people . . .

Then here on earth, the church must learn to include, welcome, and learn from those different from us, and to celebrate the unique and diverse gifts each will bring.

If in heaven children are those nearest the throne who do continually see the face of the Father . . .

Then here on earth, Christian people must use every means at our disposal to put to an end the neglect, exploitation, and abuse of Christ's little ones.

If in the peaceful kingdom of heaven, "all will sit under their own vines and under their own fig tree" and none will make them afraid . . .

Then here on earth, the children of God must take seriously the role of the peacemakers and teach the nations to study war no more.

If in heaven, Jesus found room for the thief on the cross, and offered his companion in death a place in paradise . . .

Then here on earth, a high priority must be given to a ministry to those, guilty or innocent, who are in prison, are suffering torture, or are on death row.

If in heaven the harmony of nature has been restored, the tree of life bears its fruit for all, and the leaves of the tree are for the healing of the nations . . .

Then here on earth, the human race must learn to live at peace with its environment so that everywhere will be called Eden once again.

By our own efforts we will never bring in this heavenly kingdom. Our prayer is that God in his infinite wisdom, power, and love will establish God's rule here on earth. We wait in faith and anticipation that this prayer, offered millions of times each day, will be answered. Even so, "Come, Lord Jesus."

Notes

INTRODUCTION

Kreeft, Peter. *Everything You Ever Wanted to Know about Heaven but Never Dreamed of Asking.* San Francisco: Ignatius Press, 1990.

CHAPTER ONE

Moltman, Jurgen. *The Theology of Hope.* London: SCM Press, 1967.

Lamb, Christopher. "The Legacy of Stephen Neill." *International Bulletin of Missionary Research* 2 (April 1987): 65.

Rose, Ben Lacy. "What Does It Mean to You That Jesus Is Alive." *Presbyterian Survey* 80 (April 1990): 18.

CHAPTER TWO

Donne, John. "Death" (from "Holy Sonnets"). In *Masterpieces of Religious Verse,* edited by James Dalton Morrison. New York: Harper, 1948.

Wesley, Charles. "Rejoice, the Lord is King." In *The Presbyterian Hymnal.* Louisville, Ky.: Westminster/John Knox Press, 1990.

CHAPTER THREE

Bunyan, John. *Pilgrim's Progress.* New York: Pauper Press, 1678.

Rippon, John. "How Firm a Foundation." In *The Presbyterian Hymnal.* Louisville, Ky.: Westminster/John Knox Press, 1990.

Stennett, Samuel. "On Jordan's Stormy Bank I Stand." In *The Methodist Hymnal.* Nashville: Methodist Publishing House, 1939.

Williams, William. "Guide Me, O Thou Great Jehovah." In *The Presbyterian Hymnal.* Louisville, Ky.: Westminster/John Knox Press, 1990.

CHAPTER FOUR

Barclay, William. *The Letters to the Corinthians.* Philadelphia: Westminster Press, 1960.

Bunyan, John. *Pilgrim's Progress.* New York: Pauper Press, 1678.
Handel, Georg Friedrich. *Messiah.*

CHAPTER FIVE

Hammarskjöld, Dag. *Markings.* New York: Alfred A. Knopf, 1996.
Kung, Hans. *On Being a Christian.* New York: Doubleday, 1974.
Newton, John. "Amazing Grace." In *The Presbyterian Hymnal.* Louisville, Ky.: Westminster/John Knox Press, 1990.
Yancey, Philip. *What's So Amazing about Grace?* Grand Rapids: Zondervan Publishing House, 1997.

CHAPTER SIX

Chesterson, Gilbert K. "The House of Christmas." In *Masterpieces of Religious Verse,* edited by James Dalton Morrison. New York: Harper, 1948.
Wang, Weifan. "Song of the Road Home." (Morning Prayer through Chinese Hymns, Columbia Theological Seminary, 1995).
Watts, Isaac. "Our God, Our Help in Ages Past." In *The Presbyterian Hymnal.* Louisville, Ky.: Westminster/John Knox Press, 1990.

CHAPTER SEVEN

Bunyan, John. *Pilgrim's Progress.* New York: Pauper Press, 1678.
Montgomery, James. "Well Done." In *Masterpieces of Religious Verse,* edited by James Dalton Morrison. New York: Harper, 1948.

CHAPTER EIGHT

Barclay, William. *Commentary on John 14:2–3.* Philadelphia: The Westminster Press, 1956.
Chandrakumar, M. "Heaven: What Is It? Who Will Be There?" *Decision Magazine* 31 (September 1990): 11.
Hammarskjöld, Dag. *Markings.* New York: Alfred A. Knopf, 1966.
Lewis, C. S. *The Problem of Pain.* London: Fontana Books, 1940.

CHAPTER NINE

Kittel, Gerhard. *Theological Dictionary of the New Testament.* Grand Rapids: Wm. B. Eerdmans Publishing Co., 1967.
Van De Weyer, Robert, ed. "The Celtic Psalter." In *Celtic Fire: The Passionate Religious Vision of Ancient Britain and Ireland.* New York: Doubleday, 1991.

CHAPTER TEN

Sapp, Stephen. "Living with Alzheimer's: Body, Soul, and the Remembering Community." *The Christian Century,* 21 January 1998, 54–60.

CHAPTER ELEVEN

Kittel, Gerhard. *Theological Dictionary of the New Testament.* Grand Rapids: Wm. B. Eerdmans Publishing Co., 1967.

Montgomery, James. "The Earth Is Full of God's Goodness." In *Masterpieces of Religious Verse,* edited by James Dalton Morrison. New York: Harper, 1948.

CHAPTER TWELVE

Barth, Karl. "Witness to an Ancient Truth." Interviewer unknown. *Time* (20 April 1962): 59–61.

Lewis, C. S. *Miracles.* New York: The Macmillan Co., 1947.

Moltmann, Jurgen. *The Coming of God.* Minneapolis: Fortress Press, 1996.

Pasewark, Kyle A. Review of *The Resurrection of the Body in Western Christianity,* by Caroline Walker Bynum. *The Christian Century,* 10 April 1996, 405.

CHAPTER THIRTEEN

Elwood, Thomas. In *Five Minutes a Day,* edited by R. E. Speer. Philadelphia: Westminster Press, 1943.

Lewis, C. S. *Letters to Malcolm.* New York: Harcourt, Brace, Jovanovich, 1973.

CHAPTER FOURTEEN

Browning, Robert. In *Five Minutes a Day,* edited by R. E. Speer. Philadelphia: The Westminster Press, 1943.

Newton, John. "Safely through Another Week." In *The Hymnbook.* Richmond, Va.: Presbyterian Church in the U.S., 1955.

Whittier, John Greenleaf. "Dear Lord and Father of Mankind." In *The Presbyterian Hymnal.* Louisville, Ky.: Westminster/John Knox Press, 1990.

Wordsworth, Christopher. "O Day of Rest and Gladness." *The Hymnbook.*

CHAPTER FIFTEEN

Bonnell, John Sutherland. *I Believe in Immortality.* New York: Abingdon Press, 1959.

Bunyan, John. *Pilgrim's Progress.* New York: Pauper Press, 1678.

Kipling, Rudyard. "L'Ennoi." In *Masterpieces of Religious Verse,* edited by James Dalton Morrison. New York: Harper, 1948.

Richardson, Donald W. *The Revelation of Jesus Christ.* Richmond, Va.: John Knox Press, 1964.

CHAPTER SIXTEEN

Knapp, George I. In *Five Minutes a Day,* edited by R. E. Speer. Philadelphia: The Westminster Press, 1943.

Rosetti, Christina. In *Five Minutes a Day.*

Shephard, Anne H. "Children's Hymn." In *Bible School Hymnal,* edited by I. H. Meredith and Grant Colfax Tullar. New York: Tullar-Meredith Co., 1907.

CHAPTER SEVENTEEN

Bonnell, John Sutherland. *I Believe in Immortality.* New York: Abingdon, 1959.

Bunyan, John. *Pilgrim's Progress.* New York: Pauper Press, 1678.

Ellerton, John. In *Five Minutes a Day,* edited by R. E. Speer. Philadelphia: The Westminster Press, 1943.

Stevenson, Robert Louis. "Resurgence." In *Masterpieces of Religious Verse,* edited by James Dalton Morrison. New York: Harper and Brothers, 1948.

Wilcox, E. W. In *Five Minutes a Day.*

CHAPTER EIGHTEEN

Barclay, William. *The Letter to the Hebrews.* Philadelphia: The Westminster Press, 1957.

How, William Walsham. "For All the Saints." In *The Hymnbook.* Richmond, Va.: Presbyterian Church in the U.S., 1955.

Russell, Jeffrey Burton. *A History of Heaven.* Princeton, N.J.: Princeton University Press, 1997.

CHAPTER NINETEEN

Bonar, Horatius. "Here, O My Lord I See Thee Face to Face." In *The Hymnbook.* Richmond, Va.: Presbyterian Church in the U.S., 1955.

"Brigid's Feast." In *Celtic Fire: The Passionate Religious Vision of Ancient Britain and Ireland,* edited by Robert Van De Weyer. New York: Doubleday, 1991.

CHAPTER TWENTY

Saint Augustine of Hippo. In *Christian Prayer: The Liturgy of the Hours.* New York: Catholic Book Publishing Co., 1976.

Knowles, Rex. "Before the Land." *Monday Morning* (June 1993).

Lewis, C. S. *The Problem of Pain.* London: Fontana Books, 1940.

CHAPTER TWENTY-ONE

Bernard of Clairvaux. "Jesus, the Very Thought of Thee." In *The Presbyterian Hymnal.* Louisville, Ky.: Westminster/John Knox Press, 1990.

Kreeft, Peter. *Everything You Ever Wanted to Know about Heaven but Never Dreamed of Asking.* San Francisco: Ignatius Press, 1990.

Lewis, C. S. *Miracles: A Preliminary Study.* London: The Centenary Press, 1947.

Marty, Martin. "Does Heaven Exist?" Interview by David Van Biema. *Time.* (24 March 1997):78.

Matheson, George. "O Love That Wilt Not Let Me Go." In *The Presbyterian Hymnal.*

Thomas à Kempis. "Of the Wonderful Effect of Divine Love." In *The Imitation of Christ.* New York: Grosset & Dunlap, n.d.

Wesley, Charles. "Hymn to Joy." In *The Presbyterian Hymnal.*

CHAPTER TWENTY-TWO

Bowie, W. Russel. "The Holy City." In *The Presbyterian Hymnal.* Louisville, Ky.: Westminster/John Knox Press, 1990.

Russell, J. B. "Does Heaven Exist?" Interview by David Van Biema. *Time.* (24 March 1997):77.

van Dyke, Henry Jackson. "Hymn to Joy." In *The Presbyterian Hymnal.*

CHAPTER TWENTY-THREE

Studdard-Kennedy, G. A. "Is It a Dream?" In *Masterpieces of Religious Verse,* edited by James Dalton Morrison. New York: Harper and Brothers, 1948.

Brandt, Willy. *North South: A Program for Survival.* Report of the Independent Commission on International Development Issues. Cambridge: MIT Press, 1980.

CHAPTER TWENTY-FOUR

Bernard of Cluny. "Jerusalem the Golden." In *The Hymnbook.* Richmond, Va.: Presbyterian Church in the United States, 1955.

CHAPTER TWENTY-FIVE

Chicago, Judy. "Merger." In *The Dinner Party: A Symbol of Our Heritage.* Garden City, N.Y.: Anchor/Doubleday, 1979.

CHAPTER TWENTY-SIX

Barclay, William. *The Revelation of John,* vol. 2. Philadelphia: The Westminster Press, 1960.

CHAPTER TWENTY-SEVEN

Barclay, William. *The Revelation of John,* vol. 2. Philadelphia: The Westminster Press, 1960.

How, William Walsham. "For All the Saints." In *The Presbyterian Hymnal,* Louisville, Ky.: Westminster/John Knox Press, 1990.

Lewis, C. S. *The Problem of Pain.* London: Fontana Books, 1966.

Lindsay, Vachel. "General William Booth Enters Heaven." In *Masterpieces of Religious Verse,* edited by James Dalton Morrison. New York: Harper & Brothers, 1948.

CHAPTER TWENTY-EIGHT

Kung, Hans. *Eternal Life? Life after Death as a Medical, Philosophical, and Theological Problem.* New York: Doubleday & Co., 1984.

CHAPTER TWENTY-NINE

Aquinas, Thomas. "Adoro Te Devote, Latens Deitas." In *With One Voice: A Hymnbook for the Churches,* translated by James Russel Woodford. London: Collins Liturgical Publications, 1979.
Confucius. *The Analects.* Translated by James Legge. Hong Kong: Hong Kong University Press, 1960.
Hammarksjöld, Dag. *Markings.* Translated by Leif Sjoberg and W. H. Auden. New York: Alfred A. Knopf, 1966.
Lewis, C. S. *The Problem of Pain.* London: Collins: Fontana, 1940.
Tennyson, Alfred Lord. "Crossing the Bar." In *Masterpieces of Religious Verse,* edited by James Dalton Morrison. New York: Harper and Brothers, 1948.

CHAPTER THIRTY

Bowie, Walter Russell. *Christ Be with Me.* New York: Abingdon Press, 1958.
Calvin, John. *Institutes of the Christian Religion.* Philadelphia: Presbyterian Board of Christian Education, 1936.
Kreeft, Peter. *Everything You Ever Wanted to Know about Heaven but Never Dreamed of Asking.* San Francisco: Ignatius Press, 1990.
Stewart, James S. *The Strong Name.* Grand Rapids: Baker Book House, 1972.

CHAPTER THIRTY-ONE

Kreeft, Peter. *Everything You Ever Wanted to Know about Heaven but Never Dreamed of Asking.* San Francisco: Ignatius Press, 1990.
Kung, Hans. *Eternal Life? Life after Death as a Medical, Philosophical, and Theological Problem.* New York: Doubleday & Co., 1984.